Quilts
Unfinished Stories with New Endings

GYLEEN X. FITZGERALD

FPI Publishing

Sunflower Surround ❖ 93" x 93" ❖ QUILTED BY: Beth Hanlon-Ridder

Quilts

Unfinished Stories with New Endings

GYLEEN X. FITZGERALD

Kathleen —
Tell your story!
Gyleen xxx
10/13

Quilts: Unfinished Stories with New Endings

BY: Gyleen X. Fitzgerald

FPI Publishing

P.O. Box 247
Havre de Grace, MD 21078
www.ColourfulStitches.com

BOOK DESIGN: Brian Boehm, *iDesign Graphics*

COVER DESIGN: Brian Boehm, *iDesign Graphics*

PATTERN LAYOUT: Jean Ann Wright

EDITOR: Jean Ann Wright

PHOTOGRAPHY: Dusten Wolff

STUDIO PHOTOGRAPHY: Conrad D. Johnson

PHOTO STYLIST: Beth Hanlon-Ridder

ANTIQUE CURATOR: Barbara Herron

COPY EDITOR: Barbara Polston

ISBN: 978-0-9768215-0-2

LIBRARY OF CONGRESS CONTROL NUMBER: 2008907830

Publisher's Cataloging-In-Publication Data
(Prepared by The Donohue Group, Inc.)

Fitzgerald, Gyleen X.
   Quilts : unfinished stories with new endings / Gyleen X. Fitzgerald.

     p. : ill. ; cm.

   ISBN: 978-0-9768215-0-2

1 Quilts--History.   2. Quilts--Conservation and restoration.
3. Quilting--Patterns.   I. Title.

TT835 .F58 2009
746.46   2008907830

Spiders in My Garden ❖ QUILTMAKER: Rhonda M. Adams ❖ QUILTED BY: Judy Hendrickson

Dedication

*To my mother for knowing when to hold
my hand and when to let go.*

Foreword

Not every book rates a foreword. The fashion today is breathless dedications to one's pet ("Muffy is my life!") or a convoluted introduction that presumes the reader needs hand-holding. In this case, neither is true. While Gyleen X. Fitzgerald and I share a love for slobbery, goofy Boxer dogs, that's the extent of the pet dedication. And there's no hand-holding here. This foreword is in the old-fashioned sense: I introduce you to the author and tell you why I think this work is worthwhile. My cards are on the table.

I first met Gyleen at a trade show. She listened to my lecture on market trends and then walked up to the stage to ask questions. Something about her struck me as exceptional and I marked Gyleen as someone to watch in the quilting industry. Her website revealed only a little more, so I subscribed to her weekly haiku service, knowing that the classic Japanese verse form of haiku is an elegant little literary package that speaks to the writer's inner person.

Gyleen has published other books but this one resonated immediately with me. She has found and finished and been inspired by the work of quiltmakers who've gone before. That has happened to me too when I've found old quilt blocks and wondered, "Who did these? What was the quilter thinking as she worked? What were her plans for finishing this piece?" You may one day find a quilter's cache in a relative's attic or happen upon some anonymous old quilt blocks in an antique shop. If you're a quilter, you will not be able to resist bringing home the unfinished work. This book will help you know what to do with these textile treasures, and it seems most fitting to celebrate this book with a haiku:

Found Quilt Blocks

Sacred threads, prized cloth
Patched, sewn and saved, patiently
Waiting for my hands.

Pepper Cory
Beaufort, North Carolina
December 2008

Preface

There were two main events that got me excited about unfinished vintage quilt tops and blocks. The first was a gift from Betty Phelps, an exceptional needlewoman and horticulturist who lives in Churchville, Maryland. I am one of the few quilters that Betty knows, so, when she was downsizing to a senior living residence, she gave me two boxes filled with "quilting stuff" belonging to her mother-in-law. Quilting stuff is a very loose term and by no means describes the wonderful treasures tucked away in the boxes. Betty's mother-in-law was Eva Mae Paugh who lived in Palmyra, Missouri. Based on her boxed legacy, she was a talented and accomplished quiltmaker. Unpacking, I discovered 100 plus quilt block clippings from the Kansas City Star starting in 1931, 200 pieces of original 1930s' fabric, a wool crazy quilt in progress, 40 plus Spider Hexagon blocks, and a partially assembled Double Irish Chain, all with handmade templates and notes. In addition, there was a stack of letters to her daughter from Eva Mae's mother who lived in Kansas City, Missouri.

The second event occurred when my dear friend and personal antique shopper, Barbara Herron, located 30 Feathered Star blocks in the back of an antique shop near Salem, West Virginia. I can still remember her whispering to me on the cell phone as we negotiated a reasonable price for the collection. By the time Barbara made her second visit to West Virginia, she was personal friends with the shop owner and had obtained 15 sets of blocks, four quilts, and three tops. The funniest part was when she called to inform me of my expenditure! And that "we" needed to return to the shop as if Salem, West Virginia was not eight hours from my house. I couldn't resist Barbara's enthusiasm over the newest acquisitions and we spent the long car ride home conceiving this book.

While all of this seems like destiny, I still needed help to get the quilts finished and set out to locate Beth Hanlon-Ridder whose machine quilting I had admired for years. Beth, with wit and creativity, provided advice as the tops were being transformed into quilts, especially about how they should be machine quilted. She pondered thread type and color and quilt density. Beth clearly had no angst when it came to machine quilting vintage textiles and shared my vision that these unfinished tops and blocks deserved to be finished. Our journey had commenced, and, finally we could see the ending.

Friends are the common thread throughout *Quilts* and there are dozens to thank. My life is interwoven with theirs and with the quiltmakers whose creativity inspired me to tell their stories.

Table of Contents

Introduction

Women are known as gatherers, nurturers, and maintainers of family and community. As quilters in 1930s, they created beauty during very tough times in the form of quilts to keep their families warm. They shared patterns like recipes; they stitched together as they cooked together. They hand penned letters to family and friends in far away places and sent emergency telegrams. They were busy and it's no wonder that some of their quilts never got finished ... left as orphans for another generation.

Today we still stay connected, but we've changed to email and text messages. We quilt together at retreats, at conventions, and on cruise ships. We live busy lives and things are basically the same, except we have longarm quilters to help us finish our quilts!

As I look at my vintage collection, I ask myself if I can produce more quilts and memories by starting from finished blocks or tops and getting them machine quilted? Can I pay homage to those quilters I so admire by finishing what they started? Is it possible to add my style of simple lines, contemporary fabric and unexpected color blending without compromising the original intent?

The rules are set. I will use only my stash of fabric contained in my studio. I will not take apart blocks or completed tops and start over because of workmanship or fabric choices. The quilts must be as functional as I believe they were conceived to be and they will be machine quilted. I'll write plausible stories in the form of letters to celebrate their lives. We will become one and journey together as a legacy for the next generation.

It's a tall order and I love challenges. Get comfy and enjoy the view as we step back in time on this journey to finishing for the future.

— GYLEEN X. FITZGERALD

Untold Stories

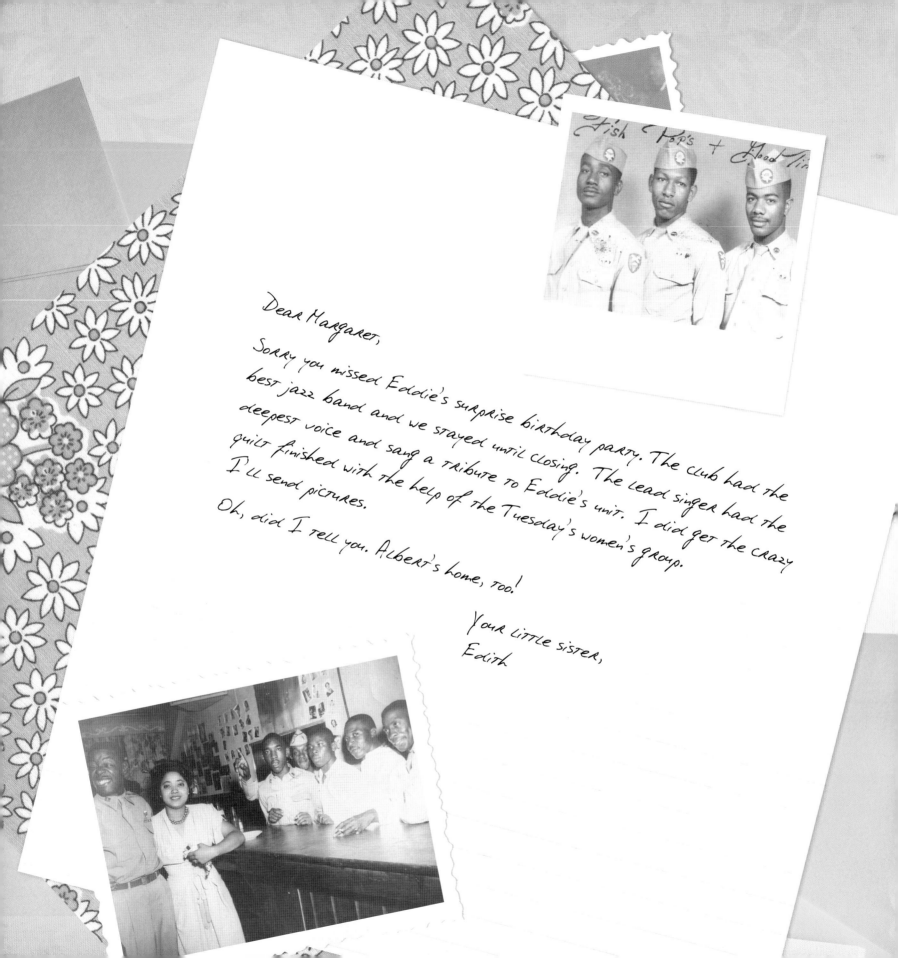

Dear Margaret,

Sorry you missed Eddie's surprise birthday party. The club had the best jazz band and we stayed until closing. The lead singer had the deepest voice and sang a tribute to Eddie's unit. I did get the crazy quilt finished with the help of the Tuesday's women's group. I'll send pictures.

Oh, did I tell you. Albert's home, too!

Your little sister,
Edith

Hot Fun in the Summertime ❖ 78" x 88" ❖ QUILTED BY: Beth Hanlon-Ridder

Grandmother's Flower Garden ❖ 70" x 82" ❖ QUILTED BY: Johanna Roll

Friendship Garden ❖ 68" x 85" ❖ Quiltmaker Unknown

With This Ring I Thee Wed ❖ 65" x 77" ❖ QUILTED BY: Gyleen X. Fitzgerald

Dear Grace,

Your father and I are so pleased with your engagement to Peter. We pray that you two will make your own way in the world, together by God's grace. Inside the box is a quilt I started so many years ago in anticipation of my own marriage. As you see, I never finished it because my hands were so busy taking care of you. It's made from my dresses that your father was fond of ... he can still remember each one. I never knew he was so particular. I hope that we will spend time together finishing it this summer in time for your wedding.

Love,
Mother

Dear Suzanne,

I can hardly keep my excitement down as I write you this letter. I just saw a beautiful Double Irish Chain made by our favorite First Lady, Mrs. Hoover. Can you imagine having a quilt just like the President's wife right in your own home? Well, I just couldn't be out done. I know that Joey will never be more than Mayor of Portland but I can pretend. Is it wrong to want what the President's wife wants? I knew you would agree, so I went ahead and started making the quilt just like hers for our house. It's going to be beautiful. When are you coming to visit? You really must meet Charles, he's dashing, single and moved to town just last month.

Roommates forever,

Phoebe

Middle Blues ❖ 73" x 82" ❖ QUILTED BY: Peg Dougherty

Crazy Ann's Clam Chowder ❖ 63" x 63" ❖ QUILTED BY: Johanna Roll

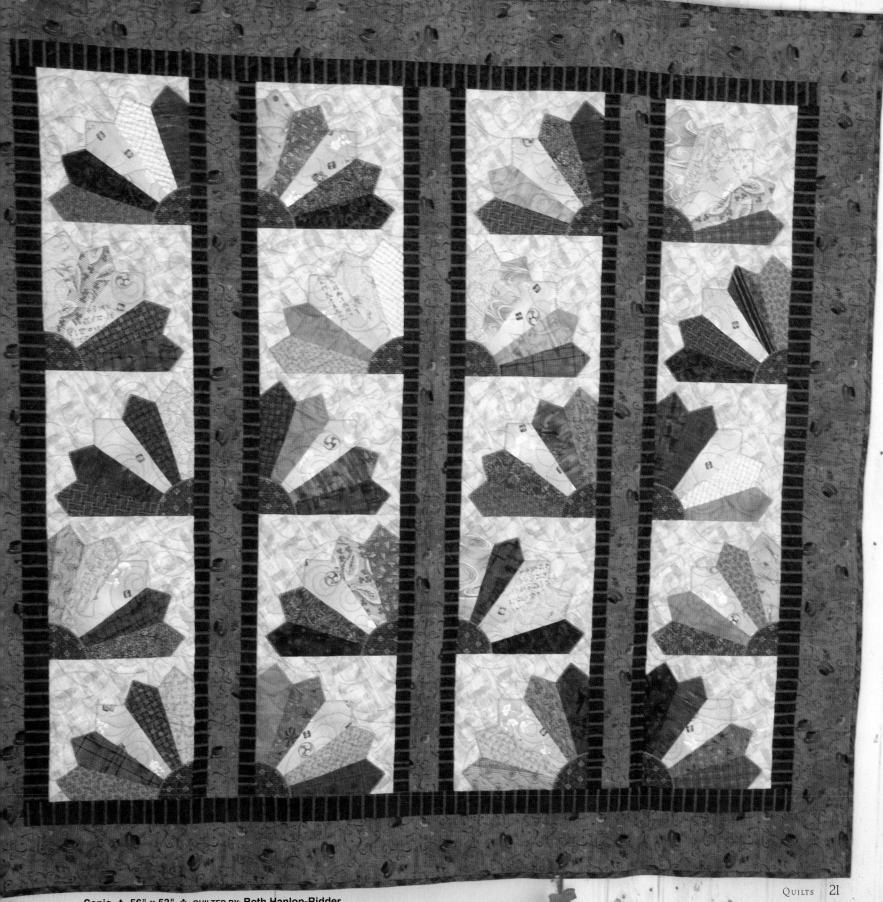

Sepia ❖ 56" x 53" ❖ QUILTED BY: **Beth Hanlon-Ridder**

Isabelle's Log Cabin ❖ 71" x 84" ❖ QUILTED BY: Johanna Roll

Dear Caroline,

It's seems like I've been gone from France forever. Thomas works long hours tending to the family's dairy farm which is more demanding than the grape orchard at home. We live in a log cabin built by his grandfather. They call it old, but it's new compared to our house in France. I've taken to quilting each night after supper and started a log cabin quilt from my old dresses. Remember the blue dress you made for me years ago? I wore it every time I was homesick. What little is left is now in the quilt. On Wednesdays, Sarah, Thomas' sister comes over to learn French. I can't understand a word she says. Miss you terribly.

Your sister,
Isabelle

Year of the Horse, 1930 ❖ 72" x 88" ❖ QUILTED BY: Beth Hanlon-Ridder

Dear Elizabeth,

Did you get the invitation for my sweet sixteen birthday party? Are you coming? You'll never believe this but Mom and Dad are finally getting me a horse ... for my birthday. Oh, the things I had to promise them to get it. You remember how embarrassing it was to learn how to ride on Tinsel, a donkey! Well I plan to go to the nationals next year so cross your fingers my new girl, takes jumps easily.

See you soon.
Josey

Cherry Blossom ❖ 62" x 62" ❖ QUILTED BY: Beth Hanlon-Ridder

Crazy Ann's Clam Chowder ❖ 63" x 63" ❖ QUILTED BY: Johanna Roll

My Darling Siler,

Be safe on the dock today. The winds are building up so take your rain slicker. I made your favorite soup, clam chowder, so you will think of me all day. It's ready to go in the thermos with the crackers. Love you and I'll be waiting to welcome you home with a kiss.

Yours truly,
Ann

Pop Pop Charron's New England Clam Chowder

2 cans of baby clams

¼ pound of salt pork,
   cut into small pieces

1 medium onion, chopped

3 potatoes, diced

3 TBS flour

1 cup milk

1 cup water

Sauté salt pork with onions and potatoes until tender. Combine flour with cup of the water blend to a smooth paste; add to soup with remaining water and milk. Stir until thickened. Add clams with the juice; heat through but do not boil. Pepper to taste. Simple ingredients and simply delicious.

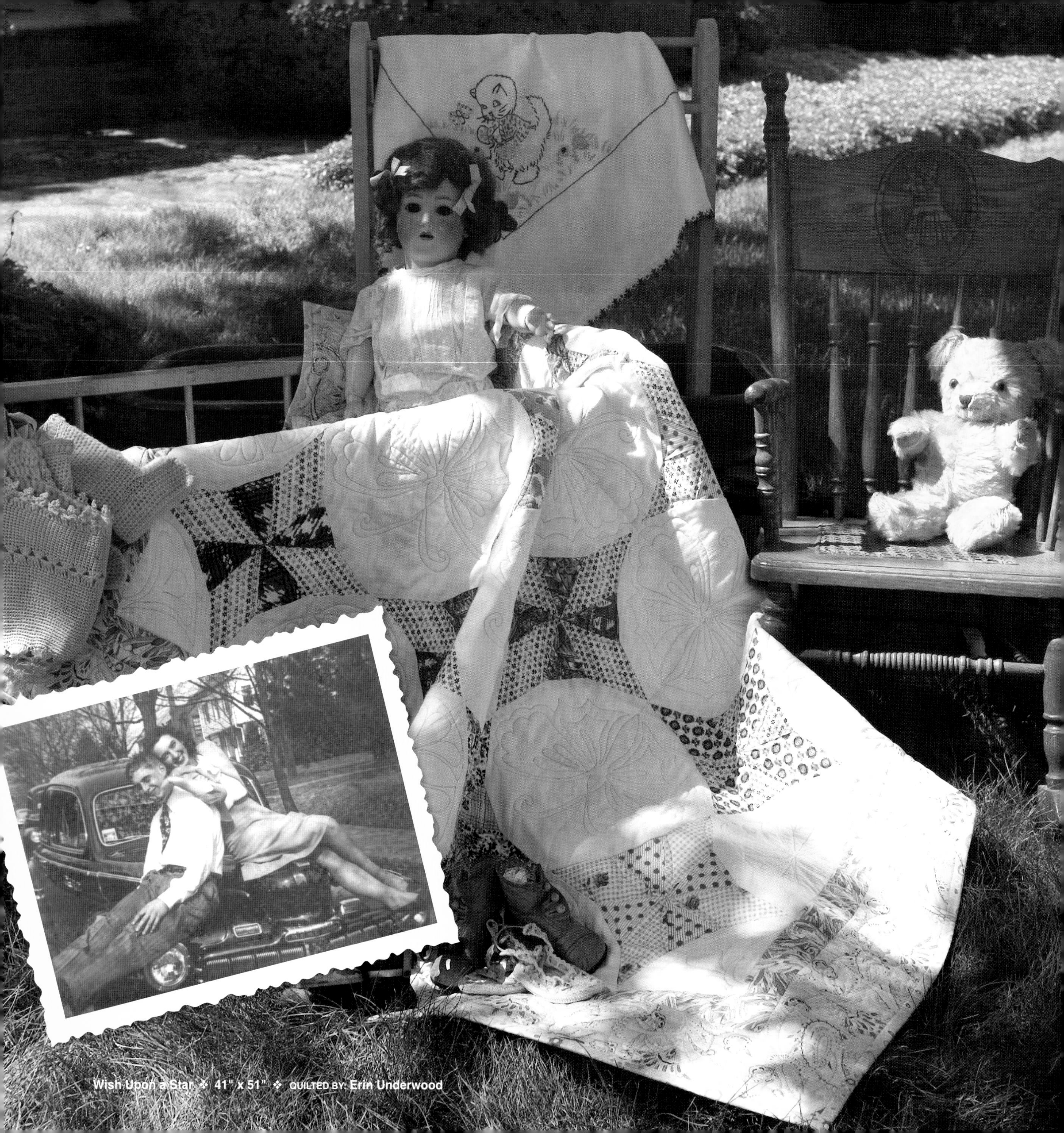

Wish Upon a Star ❖ 41" x 51" ❖ QUILTED BY: Erin Underwood

Dear Amelia,

I'm just about finished with your quilt and casting the last wish for this twelfth star. As I stitch it, I wish to give you the courage to explore your world. I know you are anxious to get out and time is almost here. You're kicking and moving all the time now. I just know you will have mother's flaming red hair, how could you not? That's why I just know you are a girl to be named after her.

Waiting for you with open arms,

Mom

Dear Jane,

Why in the good Lord's name did you leave me in charge of your garden? It's so hot and dry in Iowa; I just can't stand it. We haven't had rain since you left and I'm afraid the well's going dry. The sunflowers are so parched they refuse to look toward the sun. Everything is burnt to a crisp. I dare not utter a word to Bobby, he's working as best he can just keeping the corn from catching on fire! Tomorrow promises to be better with a thunderstorm. As I look outside I can finally see the dark clouds forming. Hurry home.

Yours truly,
Frances

Sunflower Surround ❖ 93" x 93" ❖ QUILTED BY: Beth Hanlon-Ridder

Dear Ma,

How are you and Sam coming along? Just sending you this short letter to let you know Mary had the baby. It's a boy, we named him Jacob. He's really small. Mary had a hard time of it as the baby was early. I wasn't sure either of them would make it but my boy is a fighter. Came out with fists clinched. A true McBride. Mary is coming along well. We want to thank you for the quilt. Got it Tuesday a week ago just in time.

Your son,
Jack

Jacob's Ladder ❖ **32" x 40"** ❖ QUILTED BY: Beth Hanlon-Ridder

Jack and the Beanstalk ❖ 53" x 66" ❖ QUILTED BY: Beth Hanlon-Ridder

Under the Big Top ❖ 67" x 67" ❖ QUILTED BY: Erin Underwood

Dear Bernice,

How's the big city? I just had to send you a note about all the rain we're having. I guess mother was right that it does rain when the elephants come to town. The circus came yesterday. Do you remember the fun we had as kids going to the Clyde Beatty Cole Brother Circus with Grandpa? What I remember most was the striped circus tents and eating cotton candy until my stomach hurt and of course the rain. Boy did we get rain; soaked to the bone. Those were the days.

Hugs and Kisses,
Lilly

Passage of Time ❖ 81" x 88" ❖ QUILTED BY: Erin Underwood

Tokyo Fans ❖ 68" x 63" ❖ QUILTED BY: Beth Hanlon-Ridder

Dear Mama,

Thank you for giving me your hope chest as my wedding present. It was filled with so many surprises. I was able to salvage quite a bit of the kimono fabric and decided to make a quilt. I selected a simple fan block that reminds me of the one you used on special occasions. It speaks Japan to me as I sit alone in America. Franklin was sent on another assignment so I have been praying with each stitch I take for his safe return. Please do not worry. I miss you very much.

Love,
Sumi

Dear Cousin Bessie,

It's been a long time since I've gotten a letter from you. I pray all is well and you're just busy on the farm. The girls and I are so excited. Henry has started the addition to the house and we will finally have an indoor toilet. I can say for sure right now that I won't miss the outhouse. The girls and I have started a quilt for our new living room but mostly it's to keep them out of Henry's way. I've selected a block with gentle curves remind me of Henry's saw blades. It's slow going but I'm proud of the improvement in the girls stitching. Even little Myra is piecing the blocks; her stitches are not as straight or small as Pamela's but that Myra is so strong willed. She's working all the time to be better than her big sisters.

Sincerely,
Cousin Wilhelmina

Saw Blades ❖ 74" x 74" ❖ QUILTED BY: Beth Hanlon-Ridder

Carnival ❖ 83" x 83" ❖ QUILTED BY: Beth Hanlon-Ridder

Dear Lilly,

Oh, my word how you do like to bring up old memories. Just yesterday, Deborah wanted to go to the carnival at Coney Island. My goodness what a fuss she put up until I said yes. Those rides just don't seem safe and how did we ever survive. My heart stopped dead in my chest when I saw my little girl dangling from the top of the wheel. I've aged ten years in a day. We do plan to visit by Labor Day, Lord willing!

Your sister,
Bernice

Blooming ❖ 52" x 52" ❖ QUILTED BY: Beth Hanlon-Ridder

Shooting Star ❖ 37" x 37" ❖ QUILTED BY: Gyleen X. Fitzgerald

To Finish or Not to Finish

rior to beginning this journey to finish, I was not known for restoring antique quilts or buying them. The thought that someone else's "old UnFinished Object" would enter my studio and join the zillions of my UFOs seemed silly. However, on occasion, a shopping opportunity does occur and, before I know it, I own an "old UFO"! In my house, I freely mix new with old and that includes quilts. Therefore, I'm buying with the thought to use and not just collect and store.

I stand by the presumption that a memory is not available until it is tangible and experienced. For example, you have no actual memory of a cake your mother never made; that is considered a mere thought. It doesn't matter if the cake was good or bad as long as it was made and you experienced it. Then you get a memory.

At our family gatherings, we have the most fun talking about family recipes gone bad. Every family has that one food incident that can never be lived down. There is also that dish that would make Julia Child take notes. We live them over and over again because they are wonderful memories. I want quilts to be laced through our lives in the same way.

However, to do that, to elevate them to that high pedestal, they must be finished. I will never master my mother's coconut cake and think an ingredient must be missing when I try, but I digress. Legacies are made as easily as that and I believe quilts, regardless of who started them, can do the same thing.

Let's put unfinished in perspective since not everything old is rare or valuable. I use a simple decision process to determine what to do with vintage blocks and tops. You must accept some responsibly in how you proceed as once started you can't go back to restoring its value.

If you don't like the quilt, top, or block by all means sell it or give it away. Anything pre-1900s, no matter how complete or incomplete, should be seen by a professional appraiser before you do anything. Their advice and guidance is money well spent. I do some preliminary research first to date the fabric or block design and, when lucky, to determine the area of its origin. I had a lovely collection of Birds in the Air blocks that were given to me, which I gifted to an appraiser after I discovered they were pre-1900s. She was thrilled with the vast collection of browns and blues and I was delighted that someone would care for them. They were no longer orphans.

Quilt tops in pristine condition with exceptional piecing or appliqué should also be appraised. Even if you decide to finish them, you will be doing so with complete information and that may determine if you're quilting by hand or machine. An appraiser or quilt historian can also advise you about how to finish if you want to preserve its history. You may consider using a vintage fabric or setting that would be more likely for the block and then quilting in a manner that would be typical.

I finished what I knew to be common utility quilt tops and blocks. None were heirloom quality and none were older than the 1930s. I used only current fabric so it would be easy to distinguish the old from the new and separate the work of the original quilter from my own. My goal was to honor their work by using what I received as is and to create a cohesive finish in my style of quilt making. This is my journey.

Cherry Blossom (*back*) ❖ 62" x 62" ❖ QUILTED BY: Beth Hanlon-Ridder

The Journey to Finishing...

Friendship Gardens

The best way to start is at the beginning, that point where no work is required on your part and you are only obligated to love what has been completed…by someone else. That is exactly all that was required when I became the new owner of **Friendship Gardens**. I wouldn't go out and advertise myself as a "collector" as that would tend to add dollars to the purchase price of the quilt. Let's just call me a "quilt rescuer" that for nominal payment is willing to take a quilt off your hands. For a better visual you can compare this act of humanity equivalent to going to the shelter to get a dog. Wow, a hero. This one was beautifully hand quilted in diagonal, parallel, zig-zag lines in utilitarian style across the quilt. The backing is white broadcloth that was carried to the front to create a self binding. It was loved. I could tell because the quilt felt like butter, soft to the touch and smooth as silk.

The quilt was purchased "for me" on an antique shopping trip through West Virginia. I'm partial to scrap geometric quilts that blast with color and have complex piecing. **Friendship Garden** just delights me; it's hard to take my eyes off it. What fascinates me is the play of the solid fabric in the center of the block, that dazzling double pink forming the block's corners, and those printed feedsacks and bits and pieces of probably clothing. It's an impressive variety of fabric that I'm guessing is 1930s and 1940s or so. The quilter picked a perfect pattern to showcase her sewing skills and fabric collection. It's a functional work of art.

I decided to wash it in the machine (gasp! I can hear the air being sucked out of the room) using a fragrance-free laundry liquid and adding OxiClean® on a gentle cycle for about 10 minutes. Cold water for both the wash and double rinse and I added two Shout® Color Catchers™ just in case any of the reds, blues or double pinks decided to run. All was in reasonable shape so into the dryer it went for about 30 minutes. Of course, I was holding my breath the whole time praying for the quilt's survival. Oh my, I realize how soiled it was now that the colors are brighter. Luckily, very few of the seams needed repair. I noticed the yellowing on one edge didn't come out, but don't we all have some slight imperfection? That first night's sleep under **Friendship Garden** was wonderful!

Hot Fun in the Summer Time

Summer doesn't get any crazier than this quilt! Put on your sunglasses; it's a hot one. Who would have thought to put all those plaids together? Oh heavens, how bright can yellow get? And where did that black and white check come from? So many questions unanswered, yet I still fell in love. The quilt was all tied together with the most beautiful yellow herringbone stitch embroidery. Yes, everybody needs one crazy quilt in the house to go along with that relative you would prefer to remain nameless.

This one was hand pieced on muslin feedsack and purchased as a top with the embroidery complete. The journey was short and deliberate; I purchased a blue/red plaid for the backing of a questionable fiber content from the decorator fabric section to cool down the front. The next big decision was what type of batting. Typically, crazy quilts don't contain batting; they're heavy enough with their satin, velvet and grosgrain fabric plus foundation fabric and backing. They were used more for display than on the bed for warmth. This was the "fine" ladies venue to showcase all her needlework skills. The more embroidery the better…to the point of being almost gaudy!

This top was heavy from the weight of a fairly substantial feedsack fabric. Add to that a backing that was not exactly 100 percent cotton and you could cook under the quilt. So, I selected Hobbs Thermore® batting, which is a poly blend, to lighten the load and keep it as cool as possible. It was machine quilted in a meandering pattern using yellow thread to match the punch of the embroidery. To my surprise, the thread just blended in; this was indeed one hot quilt. The final touch was a canary yellow fabric with small red motifs for the binding. Voila, finished, and everything looks like it belongs. Next!

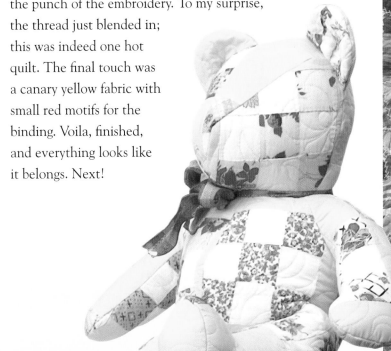

Grandmother's Flower Garden

Grandmother's Flower Garden is a classic that is usually hand pieced with precision. All those itty-bitty hexagons, it's no wonder some didn't get finished; it just took too long. Life must move on, yet this was the dream quilt to demonstrate that you had the patience of Job, so it was a popular undertaking. If you're not going to attempt this Herculean task than I suggest you look for one to buy. It's money well spent.

The quilt came to me as a top. Upon inspection the muslin seemed thin, but not necessarily weak. Now the $100 question; is it durable enough to be machine quilted? Perhaps, but it may need some help. I decided to break with tradition and add a fourth layer. I purchased a bolt of extra-wide, white muslin and used it as a layer between the quilt top and batting.

My theory is, if you don't put strain on the top while loading it on a commercial longarm quilting frame, what harm could come? And if a seam comes loose later, after washing, you would not breach the integrity of your quilt.

The quilt would still be fully intact, no batting peeking out, because the batting is sandwiched between layers of "new" fabric. It worked with the benefit of helping the original muslin appear thicker and richer, plus, the seam allowances didn't shadow through the quilt.

Another major decision when considering machine quilting is the thread color. Thread reads darker, heavier, or lighter than you want when you use the standards for selecting hand quilting thread. In hand quilting you get a dot-dash effect which softens and minimizes the thread's impact. In machine quilting, the thread lays a continuous unbroken line and can be quite dominant. So white thread was out, even though most of the fabric was muslin. I went with a soft yellow so I would see texture on the muslin and the thread would blend in when crossing the print fabric. Now, to add my touch to the finish, I selected a retro dot print cut on the bias for the binding.

I didn't attempt to wash the quilt until it was finished. The hand piecing and the thinness in the muslin were too daunting for me to overcome. The quilt had two yellowish stains that really weren't distracting, but why not try to remove them? I machined washed the completed quilt using a fragrance free laundry liquid and adding OxiClean® on a gentle cycle for about 10 minutes. I used cold water for both the wash and double rinse. Although the fabrics in this quilt are 1930s' pastel, I still thought it was smart to add two Shout® Color Catchers™, just because. Then it went into the dryer. The stains are still there, but are hard to find, and the colors came out very bright as did the muslin. Another one done.

With this Ring I Thee Wed

A **Double Wedding Ring** in mint condition; what a find! This one came from West Virginia. The quilter used old gold and blue in Four Patch units to link the rings and provide a clue to the quilt's pedigree; those are West Virginia state colors. The bits and pieces that form the rings appear to be clothing fabric; certainly not all of it was 100 percent cotton. This is a quilt I would not have made myself, love it yes, but it does look tedious. It was hand and machine pieced and already marked in the large beige areas; it was ready for quilting. My preference was to have it machine quilted. However after consultation with several long-arm quilters, it was unrealistic to expect perfection in following the marked pattern.

I didn't give up; I soaked the top in OxiClean® for three days, changing the water each day in an attempt to remove or lighten the markings. Better, but not fully removed. The quilt top was rinsed in the washer with cold water and air dried flat on the floor on top of cotton batting. I ironed it lightly then stepped back and marveled at the variety and brightness of the fabric and the workmanship of the stitching. This one was going to be hand quilted. Yes it was daunting, but I got help. Two very generous quilters, Jeanne Foster and Joan Hopkins, stitched with me and in one full calendar year, almost to the date, it was done. Whew! It's beautiful.

Middle Blues

Two-color quilts are at opposite ends of the spectrum from scrap quilts. In two colors, simplicity turns to elegance. **Double Irish Chain** is a great beginner's quilt. It's really two blocks, twenty-five small squares and one huge square with corner blocks, alternating. The fabric collection of mid-blues reminds me of Blue Willow China; it's just a stunning color twosome. Its maker lived in Austin, Texas, but I'm jumping ahead. This quilt's story started before this book was conceived and the journey to my house was completely serendipitous.

Suzanne Lupton of Portland, Oregon was visiting her sister, Linda Hoops, in Austin, Texas, when the topic of quilts came up. From what I gathered, Linda and her husband had just purchased his parents' family home and inherited, with its purchase, a trunk in the attic. That trunk contained several quilt tops, yet no one in his family quilted or knew how they got there or knew the quiltmaker. The two sisters discussed what to do with them, since neither was interested in these particular quilts, and my name came up. You see, I was the only quilter that Suzanne knew, lucky me. I was in seventh heaven when the box arrived. What is it about quilts that just make you want to rub them gently or follow each seam? **Middle Blues** was in that box; who knew it would end up finished and in a book! Blessings.

I replaced one of the 25 patches with fabric in my stash and even I have a hard time finding "my block." The one removed had a blue that I was sure would run to the end of the world, forever. Quilts of the late 1800s through the 1940s didn't always have a border like we tend to "always" do now. To have yardage for a border said something about the wealth of the maker so it was common to see quilts without borders or quilts with pieced borders. I stuck with tradition and didn't add a border on what I'm sure was a utilitarian bed quilt. Now the most troubling challenge is what color thread to use for quilting? White is too white on the blues and blue is too blue on the white. I decided to use a soft, dusty blue to just give a hint of definition to the quilting without being over powering on the white. Worked like magic.

But the story doesn't end here; years later I received another gift, this time from Betty Phelps in Churchville, Maryland. In that box was another two-color **Double Irish Chain**, 1930s' puke green

and cream in various stages. A quarter was complete, some 25 patches finished, lots more cut and yardage that I'm assuming will finish the top. That's wonderful. However, what set this particular top apart is the *Needlecraft the Magazine of Home Arts,* dated 1929 turned to an article about Mrs. Hoover, the President's wife, and her acquisition of a green and beige **Double Irish Chain**. The article included the instructions to make the quilt and Eva Mae Paugh's notes. Eva Mae is the quilter who started the one that I now own. Notes are penned in the margins. Double Blessings.

Isabelle's Log Cabin

A quilt collector has lots of quilts, yet, when asked which is their favorite, for me the answer is, "the one that I saw last." I hate to pick, yet I have not come up with a reasonable explanation why I own or make so many log cabin quilts. Would that make me a closet **Log Cabin** collector? I found this quilt on the second trip to West Virginia.

It really isn't much to look at with mostly white base, print fabric opposite white solid fabric. What strikes me as intriguing is the brilliant blue logs sparsely used. What is up with that? Using scraps of scraps? It is by far the prettiest fabric in the whole top. I bought it; it had my name on it.

Now for instructions on how to "really" kill something that is not quite dead. I decided the smart thing to do was to wash it first, in the machine of course, on the regular cycle with hot water. How could a mere 10 minutes in the washing machine turn my **Log Cabin** top into a knot of thread? Wouldn't you need more time to go from fabric to thread? It's not quite that bad, but I'll never do it again with any unfinished textile. Upon removing my **Log Cabin** from the washer, I literally used scissors to cut the thread knots on the back in order to release the top from the tangled web. Of course seams were "ripped" open and so was my heart. I let the top air dry on batting, flat on the floor, ironed it gently and started to repair all the open seams. It was my fault the top was in this condition and I was determined to make things right; this was serious! I added a cadet blue thin border and followed it with a generous black and white toile. I sleep in peace.

The Year of the Horse, 1930.

Truth be told, I appreciate appliqué quilts more than I make them. I call this pattern **Simple Flower**; it's pure without much fuss. What caught my eye is the beautiful and even hand embroidery, blanket stitch in black perle cotton, around each petal and center. The flowers are appliquéd to a heavy course feedsack that almost looks like raw linen. The palette of white base, purple, brown, black, red, and green 1930s' prints is perfect; not a lot of variety, but entertaining by being uncluttered. The top was purchased from an antique shop in Wilkes-Barre, Pennsylvania and came with a muslin backing. I replaced the eight inch muslin border with a whimsical black-base fabric of Chinese Zodiac chopsticks to give the appliqué center stage.

Crazy Ann's Clam Chowder

And then there are stacks of quilt blocks that are just waiting as orphans to be transformed into a beloved quilt. That was the case for **Crazy Ann's Clam Chowder**, a collection of 24 blocks made from a delightful assortment of mostly blue, purple, and black shirting fabric or it could have once been a real shirt. That's a plausible story since West Virginia has quite a few clothing mills and for sure bags and bags of scraps were available for pennies or free for the hauling.

One block was so poorly made, and in an absolutely hideous color grouping, that I just couldn't make myself use it. Perhaps it was a "training" block made by a beginner or child, but it was clear to me whoever made it didn't make the rest of the collection. To maximize the use of the remaining twenty-three blocks, I made two blocks from my stash fabric to get to a five by five block setting. From there it was a piece of cake, border and border and one more border. Actually, the last two borders could have been one if I had enough yardage in my stash. I was determined to use what I had on hand to push my creativity as I met each new challenge to finish the quilt. Therefore, the last two fabrics are very close in color and value so they would read as one in the quilt.

Somewhere along the way the coloring reminded me of an exceptional bowl of clam chowder from New England. I look at color in everything. I make a mental filing of color combinations for future quilts and my food is not exempt. Karen Charron and I both love winter soups. In describing this quilt to her over the phone, she agreed it would indeed have the coloring of clam chowder. Still need proof? Pop-Pop Charron's secret recipe for New England Clam Chowder appears on page 29. Make the soup and you, too, will see what I mean when you look at the color and compare it against the quilt's palette. Enjoy!

Sepia ❖ 56" x 53" ❖ QUILTED BY: Beth Hanlon-Ridder

Wish Upon a Star

Beautiful Star is the name of this pattern. It's delightful and happy on the one side yet there are not very many blocks to the collection. The fabric looks like today's retro collections, but my guess its 1940s or 1950s. Were these left over blocks or practice blocks or all that was ever made? Why stop so short at twelve?

I redrafted this pattern and discovered that with today's technology, you would still need to use templates! The antique blocks were in pristine condition, perfectly pieced and all the same size. I ignored the slight yellowing on the blocks' edges, which added character. I decided to consider this a baby's quilt and pieced the blocks together without sashing to keep the quilt as small as possible. Next came a narrow border to frame the center and I followed that with a retro paisley.

Once the top was complete, it was obvious to me that the open beige area just begged for custom machine quilting. Using neon green rayon thread and Janie Donaldson's book, *Add a Line Continuous Machine Quilting*. Erin Underwood made beautiful butterflies emerge. It's nice to add just a bit of whimsy.

I washed the completed quilt in two teaspoons of Orvus® Paste and a small amount of laundry liquid with a Shout® Color Catcher™ and then dried with medium heat.

Sunflower Surround

Let me confess that I don't buy yardage and, up to this point in the finishing process, I owned all the fabric needed to complete each quilt... until I started **Sunflower Surround**. It was, I'm not kidding you, a 22 inch block. The collection, comprised of 16 unfinished sunflower blocks, was made from an incredibly large stash of 1930s' fabric. Half were machine stitched to muslin and half were just rings of petals. None had centers. The center was basically a huge eight inch hole in the middle in the ring.

Yes, I was challenged on this one. Not that it was going to be technically difficult, but where was all that background fabric coming from? I felt like I was making a quilt for Paul Bunyan. It was time to change the rules. I must go shopping. This was daunting. How much is wrong judgment going to cost me since I needed seven yards?

The solution was to first audition fabric from my stash for color to narrow down the choices. With such a variety of medium tone, 1930s' fabric in each sunflower, I was almost positive I needed a background that read white. The next thought was scale, since I usually don't use solids. That led to more auditioning. Now what fabric do I use to fill that big hole? Intuitively, I tried a black and white print to calm things down. That usually works, but, not this time. So, what about mixing things up as in "the more the merrier?"

I finally settled on a busy, red, Japanese print that added richness and texture. It was at that point that I went shopping for the background fabric. And the winner is...retro dots. They added movement and just made me smile. I could buy seven yards if it made me smile. Done, one quilt, seven axe handles tall!

Jacob's Ladder

Baby quilt number two coming up! Ever wonder why block collections are still available? My theory is because we believe they take too much effort to finish or aren't worth finishing. The case of the twelve **Jacob's Ladder** blocks is the former. Barbara Herron saw things differently. The blocks were hand pieced and made from feedsacks. That was fine. However they also varied in size from seven to eight inches. Barbara soaked and hand washed them with OxiClean® then rinsed and let them air dry. Any thing to get me to believe they were perfect.

My first thought was to "square them up" to one size. Oops…can't cut through hand piecing like machine stitches or the whole block would fall apart. The next best thing was to mark the cutting line with pencil. That way I could place the sashing even with the marked edge and machine sew. I just didn't worry about the huge uneven seam allowances from the antique blocks. They're hidden on the inside and there are no quilt police in my studio!

The other major challenge was how to make the most of twelve very small blocks to get a reasonable-size baby quilt. The sashing helped but, in my opinion, it's the pieced border that says, "Hello, look at me and check out **Jacob's Ladder**!" I know it's a lot of piecing, but this baby is worth every stitch.

The finished quilt was machine washed using one teaspoon of Fairfield QuiltCare Quilt Wash and Shout® Color Catcher™ on a gentle cycle and warm water, then dried for 30 minutes.

Under the Big Top

Lemoyne Star heads up my top twenty list of quilts to make or own. The geometry and piecing in the block challenges the engineering side of my brain. Prior to setting out on this journey to finish, I wasn't interested in unfinished antique blocks. When was the last time you couldn't stop thinking of one item that you didn't buy? I hate it when that happens and after three days of thinking about this eclectic assortment of 1930s' **Lemoyne Stars** blocks made from red, white, and blue feedsack prints, spotted in Delta, Pennsylvania, I bought them.

I had the whole virtual quilt in my head by the time I reached my studio. When I ran out of the red fabric for the alternating blocks, my machine came to a silent halt. What would a quilter living in 1930s do? Piece the scraps until you have enough? Select another red fabric? Both were viable options. I remembered my excitement when I discovered that one or two diamonds in the **Lemoyne Stars** blocks had been PIECED! I followed her lead, dug into the trash and started piecing. Oh, what fun. One of the red alternating squares has five seams, a record for me. Can you tell, really, now that you know? And that stripe in edgy, ice-blue brings 1930s' feedsack into the prime time of today.

Passage of Time

Plaids, checks, dotted swiss, floral feedsacks, and stripes in one quilt? Even I don't have the guts to do that. Why not, it worked! Eva Mae Paugh from Palmyra, Missouri was one talented quilter and she knew that making the centers of the **Spider Hexagon** blocks the same would bring peace to the chaos. My job was to keep the peace, so I kept the design simple.

I have several "go-to" ideas when stuck with a color decision. One such is using red or black to unify. In this case, neither worked as they were too intense and agitated the hexagons. So, I used the diluted forms of them, dusty pink and smoke gray. I absolutely love hexagons and pyramids together with their geometric, clean lines simply and perfectly pieced. Repeating the pyramids in the border gives the eye a place to rest after viewing the energy of the **Spider Hexagons**. I do think Eva Mae would be pleased.

Tokyo Fans

This block is identified as **Mary's Fan** and dated 1932 in Barbara Brackman's book, *The Encyclopedia of Pieced Quilt Patterns*. Its also one of three quilts in this book in which the blocks were not finished, adding yet another challenge.

At this point, I have a wonderful collection of 1930s' fabric from quilt to quilt, yet not one is a repeat fabric from quilter to quilter. Exactly how many prints were printed in the 1930s? This collection of 1930s' fans had all the blade edges turned and the red quarter circles were basted in place. Thank heavens.

The first task was to get them onto a background to complete the block. I selected a gray/taupe, water color rose print which, in my opinion, made them look surreal. And of course I ran out of fabric again! This time I choose to just select another fabric from my stash and cut the remaining two blocks. I'm a great fan, no pun intended, of strippy quilts from Northumberland County, England and thought, "Why not give this a try?"

This old-fashioned setting with the fans gave the quilt a Japanese-screen appearance. The wonderful red Japanese border print is of questionable fiber content. To me if feels like a knit poly/cotton and, since it wasn't too stretchy, I used it. Two thousand years from now that will probably be the only thing that survives. I like to keep the mood of the quilt clear in my mind as I'm working on it. My thoughts are reflected in this haiku;

> Oolong leaves unfurl
> In Tokyo one hot night
> Silk fans move the air.

Sawblades

It is clear why these wonderful blocks were passed over at the antique shop as they were reminiscent of the Ugly Duckling story. Barbara Herron has a knack for seeing the potential in vintage blocks. I saw them and, to be honest, they didn't excite me. On the positive side, the block was intriguing with curved piecing and a nice collection of 1940s' and, perhaps, 1950s' fabric.

The list on the negative side could go on and on, but the most obvious is the variation in block size and the condition of the edges. Someone in its history washed the blocks so all the edges were frayed pretty badly. My other thought was the blocks were made by two different quilters or at two different times.

The center apricot changes to dark cantaloupe in several of the blocks and, in those blocks, the color palette is also darker. The corner apricot fabric remains the same throughout all the blocks. The quilter used a one-eighth inch seam allowance. This increased my anxiety of how

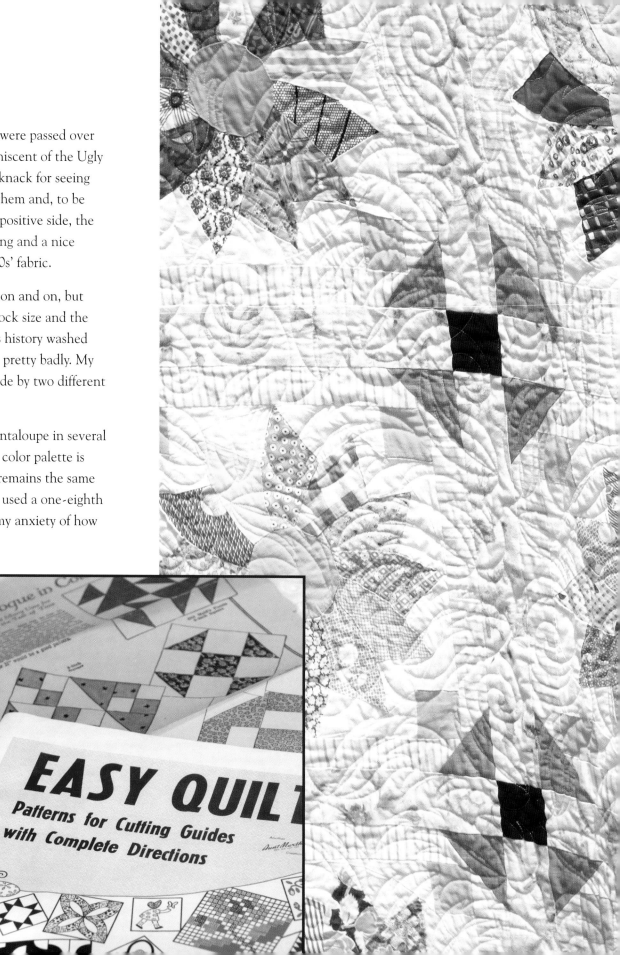

to maintain the beauty of the block and have some integrity in the finished quilt. This quilt was, by leaps and bounds, my most challenging to finish. I proceeded like a surgeon because Barbara believed the block had potential. Call it blind faith.

What I needed was a distraction, to pull the eye away from any imperfect piecing or the fact that I was getting ready to whack off blade points! I used a beige shirting stripe on all four sides of the block then followed that with a rich pumpkin tone-on-tone for corner triangles. From there, I squared the block up to a consistent size, added sashing, corner squares, and several borders. That all sounds simple enough and what was created were **Shoo Fly** blocks at the intersections! Perfect distraction. This works well because the color of the stripe and the sashing fabrics are both very close in color to the background of the **Sawblades** block so it blends adding complexity and texture. Wow, what a finish! This manly-looking quilt has emerged, is quite handsome, and no longer an Ugly Duckling.

Carnival

The **Feathered Star** block is the last to be finished but far from least in this collection. Circles can be a daunting geometric shape, and these had bias roller coaster edges that reminded me of a carnival ride. The fabric is classic 1930s, soft and in medium tones.

I went shopping again for that buttery, pastel yellow print to have the circles just blend into the background block. I machined pieced the circles into the huge hole in the background fabric and used precisely twelve straight pins to hold each of the star points in the clock positions. I eased them into the correct position and leveraged on the fact that bias edges can be manipulated. Think of it as putting a sleeve into an armhole on a garment.

From there, it was just block-to-block sewing. Oops, too boring. Yes, I unsewed and added corner triangles to each block in my "go to" red color. To keep the red from looking out of place, I added a pieced border of red triangles. Beth Hanlon-Ridder added the finishing touch by machine quilting happy swirls in yellow thread going from edge to edge across the surface of the quilt.

FEDERAL HILL
FARM

R.L. Compton, Jr.   Street, Marylan

Reflections

There are times when a few quick fixes are necessary before you can begin layering and quilting. You must examine the quilt to see if you need to make small repairs or replace some of the blocks/patches. Don't get too crazy doing this because, before you know it, you'll find yourself remaking the entire quilt top! For example, I used a hand-dyed, medium pink color to replace a flaming red "velvet" in a nine patch because I was sure the velvet would bleed forever. I re-used all remaining original patches and reassembled the block. The choice is yours to determine if you're going to hand-piece or machine piece the block when you sew it back together.

You'll probably want to check the stability of the fabric in a quilt top before it's quilted. Be warned that anything could happen, the worst being a ruined non-repairable top or block. When in doubt seek a professional opinion. The pros have all kinds of wonderful ways to clean and protect fabric, or they may just recommend that the top be left alone.

If the quilt top is thin (especially in the muslin or white areas), try adding a layer of bleached white muslin under the quilt top. This additional layer reduces stress on weak quilt tops and helps eliminate the migration of the batting through the top after quilting. If by chance a hole appears, its okay since the quilt top is no longer the structural layer. If a hole appears after the top is quilted consider covering it with a simple appliqué shape. Butterflies, hearts, or yo-yos all add whimsy to the quilt and clearly a future owner or collector will know this is a deliberate added touch.

As for the quilting, finishing means getting the quilt completed by a professional longarm quilter for two reasons. First, there just isn't enough time and second, machine quilting adds durability to any quilt that I plan to use, display, and pass on to someone else. Be careful of your choice of thread color. The wrong choice can overpower your quilt. When in doubt consult a professional machine quilter; they've seen it all. If you're going to hand quilt, get moving and start basting; without beginning the quilt will never be finished.

If you're going to wash the finished quilt, a machine without a center agitator is ideal. Use a soap specifically developed for quilts. Spread the quilt on a layer of batting on the floor or take it outside to dry. I like to do the drying outside on the grass or driveway, but out of direct sunlight, so my quilts are not washed until the weather permits.

The most important part of the process is to enjoy the journey to finishing.

Happy snuggling! Gyleen

New Beginnings

Cherry Blossom

This two-block quilt with checkerboards and alternating blocks is a rather freeing way to make a Double Irish Chain. It allows you to make a quilt with slight tone variations and show off a beautiful border fabric. I like the tight color palette as it leans towards elegance without being pretentious.

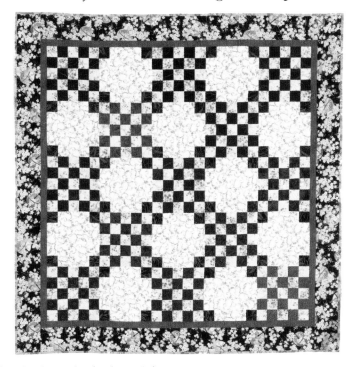

Quilt Size: 62" x 62"
Block Size: 10" x 10"
Block Count: 25
Quilted by Beth Hanlon-Ridder

Supplies:

Fabric tip: select feature fabric and setting squares from a very narrow color palette.

(13) 2-1/2" strips of dark feature fabric for checkerboard block
1 yd light print fabric for checkerboard blocks
1 yd light fabric for alternating block
1 yd bright for border #1 and binding
1 yd large print for border #2
4 yds for backing
Twin size batting
Rotary cutter, ruler and cutting mat
Neutral color cotton thread
Rayon thread for quilting

Checkerboard Blocks: Make 13

1. Cut (13) 2-1/2" x 40" strips from the light print fabric. Crosscut one of the strips into (13) 2-1/2" squares, set aside.

2. Pair up one strip of feature fabric and light print fabric. Sew together lengthwise, press seams towards the dark strip.

3. Crosscut the sewn strip into 2-1/2" segments and layout, alternating the fabrics as shown. Sew segments together. Make 2.

4. Sew two units together.

5. Sew a 5th row with two segments and one light print square.

6. Sew the row in place to complete a block.

Alternating Pieced Blocks: Make 12

7. Cut (2) 6-1/2" x 42" strips from light alternating fabric.

8. Cut (4) 2-1/2" x 42" strips from dark feature fabric. Sew a 2-1/2" dark strip to each side of a 6-1/2" wide light strip. Make 2 sets.

9. Crosscut into (24) 2-1/2" segments.

10. Cut (3) 6-1/2" x 42" strips from light fabric for alternating block. Cross cut into (12) 6-1/2" x 10-1/2" pieces.

11. Sew two segments made in steps 8 and 9 to opposite ends of 6-1/2" x 10-1/2" pieces cut in step 10. Make 12 blocks.

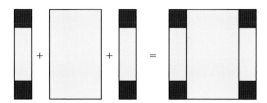

12. The quilt is sewn together in five alternating rows. There are 3 odd numbered rows and 2 even numbered rows.

Rows 1, 3 and 5

Rows 2 and 4

13. Sew the rows together to complete the center area of the quilt top.

14. Cut fabric for border #1 into (6) 1-1/2" x 42" strips. Sew the strips together end-to-end. Measure the quilt from top to bottom through the center of the quilt and cut (2) border strips equal to this measurement. Sew borders to both sides of the quilt.

15. Measure the quilt from side to side through the center of the quilt and cut (2) border strips equal to this measurement. Sew borders to the top and bottom of the quilt.

16. Cut fabric for border #2 into (6) 5-1/2" x 42" strips. Sew the strips together end-to-end. Measure, cut and sew the vertical and horizontal borders in the same manner as steps 14 and 15.

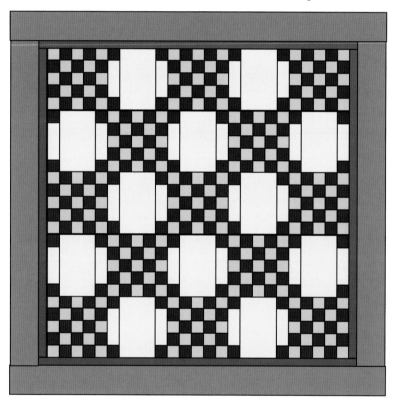

17. Layer backing, batting and quilt top. Try machine quilting using rayon thread to give your quilt a shimmering dimension and a bit of sparkle. Quilt in an overall pattern to enhance the fabrics and design of the quilt.

18. Cut bright binding fabric into (7) strips 2-1/2" x 42". Sew strips together end-to-end. Fold strip in half lengthwise and press fold line. Align raw edges of binding to raw edges of quilt top. Sew in place. Turn folded edges to back of quilt and sew in place.

19. Add label with your name and date. Add sleeve for hanging.

Blooming

Start by selecting an outstanding print for your border. Large and small prints work equally well. The border will be the basis from which you will select the fabric for the logs. I wanted my logs to simply dance as if they were flower petals so I used hand dyed fabrics. Tone-on-tone or fabrics called "blenders" will give that same appearance. Visually simplifying the quilt's center allows you to really showcase some fancy machine quilting. Beth used reddish-brown variegated thread and a detailed hibiscus pattern that plays on the flowers found in the borders.

Quilt Size: 52" x 52"
Block Size: 8" x 8"
Block Count: 25
Quilted by Beth Hanlon-Ridder

Supplies:

1-3/4 yd large floral print for border, binding and center squares

Assortment of tone-on-tone fabric or fabrics which read almost solid and remotely match your border floral print. You will need about 50 or more strips 1-1/2" x 40". The longest piece needed is 11" so scraps are also a good choice. It doesn't matter if your strips are dark, medium or light in value.

56" square quilt batting
Sewing and quilting thread
Rotary cutter, ruler and cutting mat

Log Cabin Block Sewing Tips:

Always place the log cabin block closest to your sewing machine feed dogs. Position the strips (logs) in place on top of the block. This helps keep the blocks square. Take care not to stretch the logs as you sew them in place.

As you add the logs always work in a clockwise direction to form the rounds of logs around the center square. Follow the numbering order on the diagram to add the logs. There are 3 full rounds of logs in the block. Each fabric/color is used for two consecutive logs. Try not to use the same fabric more than once in the same block. Colors can be repeated in subsequent blocks.

Trim each new log even with the block assembly after you sew. I highly recommend using 8" scissors for the cutting. Cut the strips before you fold them out to press the seams. This will keep the logs even with the block as you add each row.

Fold each log away from the block and press seam allowance towards the new log. It is important to press each seam allowance as new logs are sewn in place. Take care not to push too hard with the iron and stretch the logs as you press the seams. After the block is completed some quilters like to use spray starch for a final pressing to stabilize the block.

Instructions:

1. Cut (2) strips 2-1/2" x width of fabric strips, recut into (25) 2-1/2" x 2-1/2" squares for the center of the blocks..

2. Select a 1-1/2" strip for the first log at random. Sew the strip to a center square. Cut the strip even with the square. This is log #1. Press seams. Using the same fabric, sew a 2nd strip to the assembly as log #2. Trim to edge of block. Press.

3. Select another color strip at random. Sew the strip to the assembly as log #3 and log #4. Trim and press seams.

4. Continue adding logs for 3 full rounds around the center square. Make 25 blocks with different color arrangements..

5. Using your ruler, check the final sizes of your blocks. The finished size of the blocks should be 8-1/2" including outside seam allowances. If the blocks are only 1/8" off, don't worry about it. If they are more or less than an 1/8" off consider squaring the blocks to be all the same size.

6. Sew the blocks together in 5 rows of 5 blocks each. Play with the placement of the blocks until you achieve a color combination that is pleasing to your eye.

7. Sew the rows together to complete the center section of the quilt top. Press seams.

8. Cut fabric for border into (5) 6-1/2" x 42" strips. Sew the strips together end-to-end. Measure the quilt from top to bottom through the center of the quilt and cut (2) border strips equal to this measurement. Sew borders to both sides of the quilt.

9. Measure the quilt from side to side through the center of the quilt and cut (2) border strips equal to this measurement. Sew borders to the top and bottom of the quilt.

10. Layer backing, batting and quilt top. Quilt in an overall pattern to enhance the design of the quilt.

11. Cut binding fabric into (6) strips 2-1/2" x 42". Sew strips together end-to-end. Fold strip in half lengthwise and press fold line. Align raw edges of binding to raw edges of quilt top. Sew in place. Turn folded edges to back of quilt and sew in place.

12. Make a label to identify this quilt as being your art; add a hanging sleeve.

Year of the Horse - 1930

The quilt is simply elegant, a delicate, eight petal flower appliquéd on feed sack.
This is as easy as appliqué gets with only two templates, one for the petals and one for the center.

Quilt Size: 72" x 88"
Block Size: 12"
Block Count: 30
Quilted by Beth Hanlon-Ridder

Supplies:

Petals: 10 fat quarters (22" x 18") or assorted scraps 3" x 5"
Flower Center: 1 fat quarter solid gold
4 yd background fabric
1 yd border fabric
2/3 yd binding
#12 perle cotton for hand applique
30 weight thread; #110 needle for sewing machine applique
Heat resistant template material
Liquid starch
Cotton swabs

Instructions:

1. Trace the petal template onto heat resistant template material. Cut out at actual size. Repeat for the flower center.

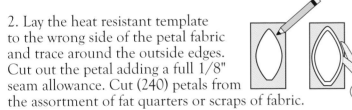

2. Lay the heat resistant template to the wrong side of the petal fabric and trace around the outside edges. Cut out the petal adding a full 1/8" seam allowance. Cut (240) petals from the assortment of fat quarters or scraps of fabric.

3. Using liquid starch and cotton swab; wet the seam allowance around the outside edges of petal.

4. Using the side of a dry iron set to medium, press each petal's 1/8" seam allowance over the edge of heat resistant template. Allow to cool and then remove the template. Repeat for all 240 petals.

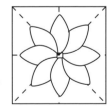

5. Cut the background fabric into (30) 12-1/2" squares. Fold in quarters then from corner to corner and press fold lines. Align each of the eight flower petals with the fold lines on the block. Pin in place.

6. Use a blanket stitch and appropriate thread to appliqué the petals to the background square by hand or machine.

7. Using the method outlined in step 2, trace 30 flower centers on the back of the fat quarter of gold fabric. Cut out the flower centers adding 1/8" seam allowance. Turn edges following the method used in step 3.

8. Position a flower center on an appliquéd flower block and blanket stitch in place. Make 30 blocks.

9. Arrange the blocks in 6 rows of 5 blocks each. Sew the blocks into rows; sew the rows together for the quilt center.

10. Cut the border fabric into (8) 6-1/2" x width of fabric strips. Sew the strips together end-to-end. Measure the quilt from top to bottom through the center of the quilt and cut (2) border strips equal to this measurement. Sew borders to both sides of the quilt.

11. Measure the quilt from side to side through the center of the quilt and cut (2) border strips equal to this measurement. Sew borders to the top and bottom of the quilt.

12. Cut (8) 2-1/2" strips for binding. Sew together end-to-end. Fold in half lengthwise and press. Pin raw edges of binding to raw edges of quilt top and sew in place. Turn folded edge to back and sew in place.

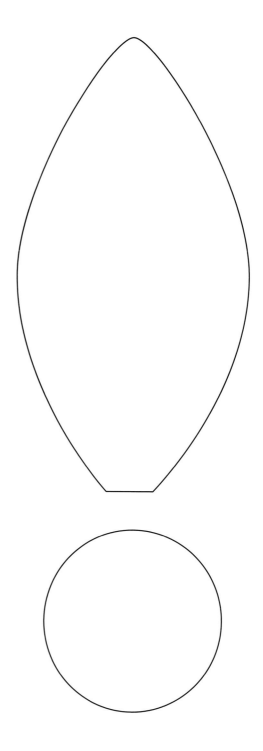

Full Size Pattern Templates

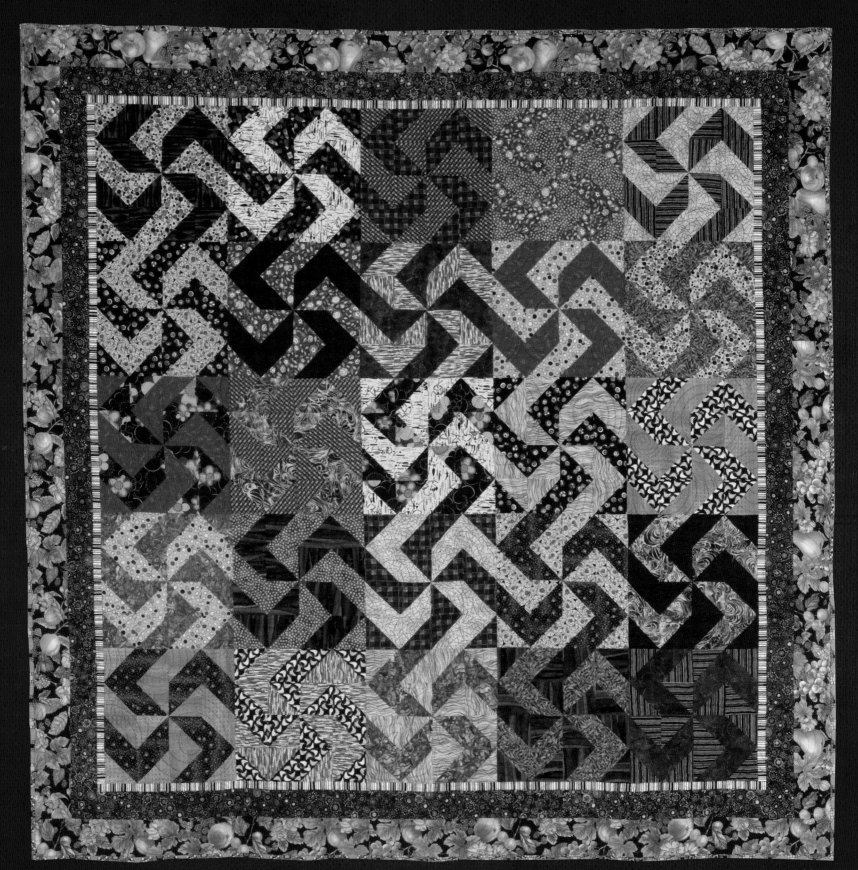

Tootie Fruitie

My love for this block started with the collection of 25 blocks pieced from very pale and delicate shirting. I turned those blocks into a lovely quilt then longed to make it again using super-saturated colors. My rendition reminds me of summer's heat and slurping Tootie Fruitie water ice.

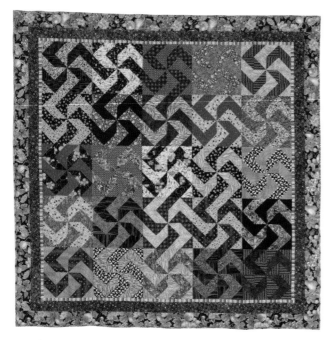

Quilt Size: 77" x 77"
Block Size: 12" x 12"
Block Count: 25
Quilted by Beth Hanlon-Ridder

Supplies:

26 fat quarters 22" x 18"
1/2 yd for border #1
1 yd for border #2
1 yd for border #3
5 yds for binding and backing
Twin size batting
Fabric Tips: I used novelty and fun fabrics to get a summer picnic feel to the quilt. As far as fabric goes the sky's the limit; try a reproduction or pastel palette from the 1930s.

Special Tool:

Easy Angle™ Ruler by Wrights or
3" finish Triangles on a Roll™ by HQS, Inc.

Instructions:

1. Using the 26 fat quarters cut (4) 3-1/2" strips from each. Divide into two piles, one with light values labeled fabric A and one with dark values labeled fabric B. Combine 2 strips of fabric A with 2 strips of fabric B for a total of 26 sets. Mix and match so that each set is different.

2. Working with one set, layer 1 of each strip (A & B) with right sides together. Using the Easy Angle Ruler, cut (16) half square triangles (HST).

3. Sew on the diagonal to form the HST. Press toward the darkest fabric.

4. Layout the HST following the diagram, the lighter of the two fabrics will form the swirl. Sew in sets to make a Four Patch. Press seams. Make 4.

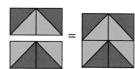

5. Follow the diagram and sew the four sets made in step 4 together to complete the block. Pressing seams in opposite diretions will keep the center flat. Make 12 blocks with the lighter of the two fabrics forming the center swirl.

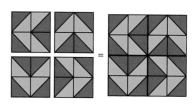

6. Make 13 blocks that put the darker of the two fabrics in the position to form the swirl. In some cases you will be choosing between two medium value fabrics, which is okay, just look for the contrast and keep making blocks.

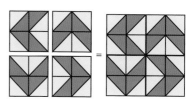

7. Arrange the 25 blocks in 5 rows with 5 blocks in each row. Start with a dark swirl block and alternate with a light swirl block. Rows 1, 3 and 5 start with the dark swirl blocks and rows 2 and 4 start with a light swirl block.

The tessellation or interlocking between the blocks should be evident yet disappear in some places. The disappearing is caused by the mediums or low contrast blocks.

8. Sew the blocks together to complete the rows. Press seams to the left in rows 1, 3 and 5. Press seams to the right in rows 2 and 4.

9. Sew the rows together from top to bottom to complete the center of the quilt top. Press seams.

10. Cut fabric for border #1 into (7) 1-1/2" x 42" strips. Sew the strips together end-to-end. Measure the quilt from top to bottom through the center of the quilt and cut (2) border strips equal to this measurement. Sew borders to both sides of the quilt.

11. Measure the quilt from side to side through the center of the quilt and cut (2) border strips equal to this measurement. Sew borders to the top and bottom of the quilt.

12. Cut fabric for border #2 into (8) 3" x 42" strips. Sew the strips together end-to-end. Measure, cut and sew the vertical and horizontal borders in the same manner as steps 10 and 11.

13. Cut fabric for border #3 into (8) 4-1/2" x 42" strips. Sew the strips together end-to-end. Measure, cut and sew the vertical and horizontal borders in the same manner as steps 10 and 11.

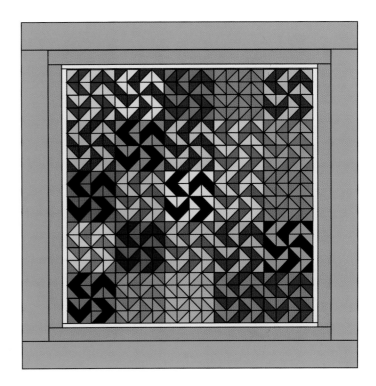

14. Layer backing, batting, and quilt top. Try machine quilting using rayon thread to give your quilting a shimmering dimension and a bit of sparkle. Another effective but quick hand quilting approach would be to use #8 perle cotton and a utility stitch. Try quilting in an overall swirling pattern to enhance the block design.

15. Cut binding fabric into (9) strips 2-1/2" x 42". Sew strips together end-to-end. Fold strip in half lengthwise and press fold line. Align raw edges of binding to raw edges of quilt top. Sew in place. Turn folded edges to back of quilt and sew in place.

16. Use the 26th block as your label. Add a 1-1/2" border to the sides of the block using a light colored fabric. Record, at a minimum, the name of the quilt, your name, receiver's name if it is a gift, the date completed, and city and state where the quilt was made.

Wish Upon A Star

This block is called Beautiful Star. I would say they are 1940s' vintage based on the fabric, but they are looking rather trendy based on today's fabric designers, proving that fabric design just goes in one big circle. You should have no problem selecting today's fabric that mimics the fabrics used so long ago.

Quilt Size: 41" x 51"
Block Size: 10"
Block Count: 12
Quilted by Erin Underwood

Supplies:

13 fat eights (9" x 18")
1 yd background fabric
1/2 yd border #1 fabric
1 yd border #2 fabric
1-1/2 yd backing fabric
1/2 yd binding
Twin Size batting

Set Up:

Using medium weight card stock (like a file folder) and glue stick, glue the templates onto the card stock. Let dry. Cut along the outside line. The inside line is your stitching line. The templates include seam allowances.

Instructions:

1. Layer 2-3 fat eights, right side down, on cutting surface and trace (4) diamond shapes and (4) triangle shapes. Cut out shapes; it is easier if you pin in the center of each shape to hold the layers together. Continue for the remaining fat eights.

2. Using the background fabric, fold right sides together, trace the wedge shape. You will need 48 wedges.

3. Sort fabric "parts" to create a set for each block with two fabrics plus the background wedge in a set. Mix and match fabric combinations to make each star block.

One set is:
(4) triangles   (4) diamonds
(4) wedges using background fabric

4. Working with one set, sew diamonds to triangles. Align tips of the diamond and triangle, sew from beginning to end. You should be able to chain stitch to complete all 4 pairs. Press seams toward the diamond. Make 4 pairs.

5. Join the pairs by sewing the diamond to the triangle to make a half star. Press seam so that all seams are in the same direction. Make 2 half stars.

6. Join the half stars matching seams at the center. Press seam open.

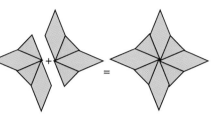

What do you think so far? Is your star twinkling?

7. Adding the wedge is next. Center the wedge across the triangle's edge. Pin the beginning and end. Sew this edge moving the seam allowance if necessary. Remove or unsew any stitches within the seam allowance. Try not to cut the stitches, just unsew. Pivot the wedge across one edge of the diamond. Pin in position and start sewing from the triangle. Sew to the end. Repeat for the other side of the diamond. Press seams. Add all 4 wedges to complete the star block. Make 12 blocks.

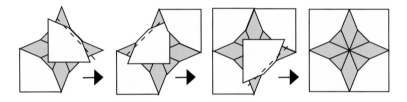

8. Arrange the blocks in 4 rows with 3 blocks in each row. Sew blocks together to form rows. Press seams to one side. Sew the rows together to form the quilt top. Press the row seams.

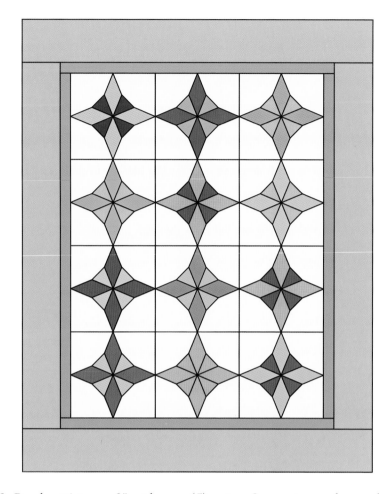

9. Border #1 is cut 2" wide; cut (5) strips. Sew strips end-to-end. Measure the length of the quilt from top to bottom. Cut (2) border strips equal to this measurement. Sew to both sides of the quilt; press toward the border.

10. Measure the quilt from side to side. Cut (2) strips equal to this measurement. Sew to both sides of the quilt; press towards the border.

11. Repeat with border #2. Border #2 is cut 4-1/2" wide. You will need (5) strips.

12. Layer the quilt backing, batting and quilt top. Baste the layers together. Try using rayon thread to add shimmer to the quilt. Erin quilted a butterfly between the blocks.

13. Cut binding fabric into (5) 2-1/2" x 42" strips. Sew together end-to-end. Fold in half lengthwise and press for a double fold binding. Match raw edges of binding to raw edges of quilt top. Stitch in place. Turn folded edge to back of quilt and stitch in place.

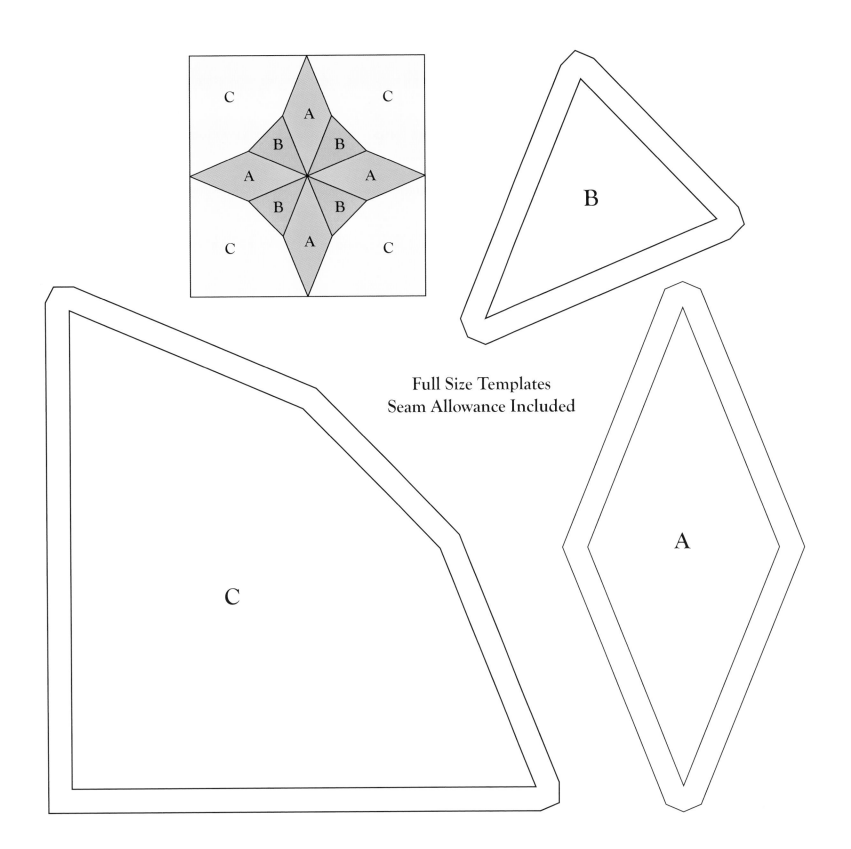

Full Size Templates
Seam Allowance Included

Jack And The Beanstalk

I used a very narrow color palette for the feature fabric. The sashing fabric was a large scale print with lots of black space. I think the whimsical flecks of color add to the movement and color balance.

Quilt Size: 53" x 67"
Block Size: 12"
Block Count: 12
Quilted by Beth Hanlon-Ridder

Supplies:

5 feature fabrics, total of 7 fat quarters
1-1/2 yd background fabric
3/4 yd for cornerstones and border #2 setting squares
1-1/2 yd for large scale print for sashing
1-1/2 yd for setting triangles for border #2
5 yds fabric for binding and backing
Twin size batting

Special Tools:

Easy Angle™ Ruler by Wrights or
4" finish Triangles on a Roll™ by HQS, Inc
Companion Angle™ Ruler by Wrights

Instructions:

1. For the Four Patch block unit cut (1) 2-1/2" x 42" strip of background fabric and (2) 2-1/2" x 22" strip of feature fabric.

Place feature fabric and background fabric strips with right sides together. Stitch lengthwise from one end to the other. Cross cut every 2-1/2" for a total of (10) segments. Sew into pairs to make a Four Patch block. Make 5.

2. For the Half Square Triangle (HST) units, cut (1) 4-1/2" x 10" strip from feature fabric and (1) 4-1/2" x 10" strip from backbround fabric.

Place 1 strip of background fabric with 1 strip of feature fabric, right sides together. Using the Easy Angle Ruler, cross cut for (4) triangles. Sew each pair together on the diagonal (long side). Press seam to one side. Make 4.

3. Lay out the 5 Four Patch units and 4 HST units. Sew the units to form 3 rows, then sew the rows together to form the Jacob's Ladder block.

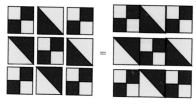

Repeat steps 1 through 3 for the remaining 11 blocks.

4. For the sashing, cut (6) 2-1/2" x 42" strips. Cross cut into (17) 2-1/2" x 12-1/2" sashings.

5. Cut (6) 2-1/2" x 2-1/2" squares from the cornerstone fabric.

6. Stitch 3 sashing rows using 2 cornerstones and 3 sashing strips. Press seams toward sashing segments.

7. Add sashing segments to the sides of the Jacob's Ladder block to form rows. Press seams toward sashing. Every other row starts with the block turned in the opposite direction. Make 4 rows of blocks. Alternate the block rows and sashing rows and sew the rows together.

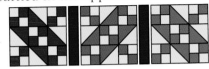

8. Using the fabric for border #2 setting square fabric, cut (5) 3" x 42" strips. Cross cut for (64) 3" x 3" squares.

9. Cut (6) 3" x 42" strips from setting triangle fabric. Cross cut (136) triangles using the Companion Angle Ruler.

10. Sew a triangle to opposite sides of each setting square. Press seams toward the triangle.

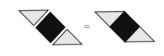

11. Sew segments in a row with 17 setting squares for the side borders. Make 2.

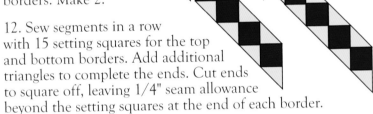

12. Sew segments in a row with 15 setting squares for the top and bottom borders. Add additional triangles to complete the ends. Cut ends to square off, leaving 1/4" seam allowance beyond the setting squares at the end of each border.

13. To make a perfect fit based on your quilt, lay the quilt top and border sections on a flat surface. Measure the following:

Dimension A: measure the quilt from top to bottom.
Dimension B: measure the length of one side of border #2.
Dimension C: measure the quilt from side to side.
Dimension D: measure the length of top/bottom border #2

14. At this point it is easier not to think about it, just do it.

The width of border #1. (D minus C minus 6"), divided by 2 = _____ . This is cut width E.

Using border #1 fabric cut (4) strips using width E. Sew strips end-to-end. Cross cut (2) strips A long. Sew to the sides of quilt top. Press towards border #1.

The width of border #1 (B minus A plus 1") divided by 2 = _____. This is cut width F.
Measure the quilt from side to side (quilt plus both side border #1 strips). This is length G. Cut (3) strips using width F. Sew strips end-to-end. Cross cut (2) strips G long. Sew to top and bottom of the quilt. Press towards border #1.

15. Sew border #2 long pieced strips to each side of the quilt. Press seams towards border #1. Sew the border #2 short pieced strips to the top and bottom of the quilt and press seams toward border #1 to complete the quilt top.

16. Layer the quilt backing, batting, and quilt top. Baste the layers together. Quilt as you like. Beth quilted mine on a longarm machine using a paisley pattern. The thread was a variegated purple to red blend.

17. Cut remainder of backing/binding fabric into (7) 2-1/2" x 42" strips. Sew together end-to-end. Fold in half lengthwise and press for a double fold binding. Match raw edges of binding to raw edges of quilt top. Stitch in place. Turn folded edge to back of quilt and stitch in place.

Border Measuring Diagram

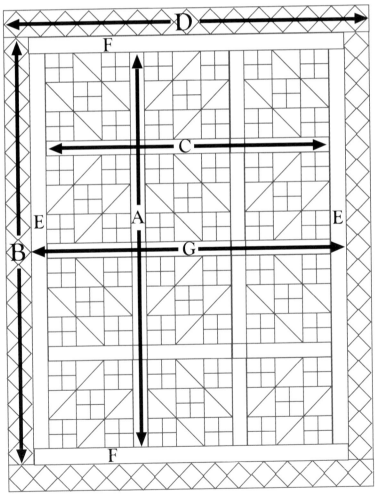

Shooting Star

I'm in heaven! Diamonds, squares and triangles...three fun geometric shapes in one quilt!
It works like a puzzle and is pieced from the outside in. Makes you take pause in the extraordinary
math skills of those 1930s' ladies. If they could do it, so can you!

Quilt Size: 37" x 37"
Block Size: 7-1/4" x 7-1/4"
Block Count: 9
Quilted by Gyleen X. Fitzgerald

Supplies:

8 fat eighths (18" x 11") for star points
1 fat quarter (22" x 18") star background
1 fat quarter for setting squares
1/2 yd for setting triangles
1-1/4 yd for border and binding
1-1/4 yd backing fabric and craft size batting
Rotary cutting supplies, straight pins and seam ripper

Special Tools:

Companion Angle™ Ruler by Wrights
45 and 60 Degree Diamond Ruler by Creative Grids™

Instructions:

1. Using the star background fabric, cut (36) 2-1/2" squares. Cut 2" x 22" strips and cross cut (36) quarter squares triangles using the Companion Angle Ruler.

2. Using star point fabric and 45 and 60 Degree Diamond Ruler cut the diamonds for the Lemoyne Star. Align fabric dge with the notation that says (2" finished side/edge) on the ruler at the 45° end. Use the ruler for the guide and cut across the full 22" width of fabric (wof). Cross cut diamonds from each strip. Cut (1) strip from each to start and cut the remaining strips as needed to finish all 9 stars.

3. Each block uses 2 fabrics for the 8 star points with (4) 45° diamonds from each fabric.
Make 36 "star sets" by stacking and pinning together:
(4) 45° diamonds, fabric A   (4) 45° diamonds, fabric B
(4) 2-1/2" squares, background fabric
(4) quarter square triangles, background fabric

4. Using one set, sew short leg of quarter square triangle to top right side of fabric A diamond. The alignment will not be perfect; the triangle will end at the edge of the diamond. Press seam toward diamond.

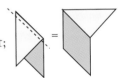

5. Sew remaining short leg of quarter square triangle to top left side of fabric B diamond. Sew straight into the seam allowance. You should also have the same overlap as in step 4. Press seam toward diamond. Un-sew all stitches in the seam allowance.

6. Fold quarter square triangle in half (wrong sides together) with the diamonds on top of each other and in perfect alignment. Sew bottom diamond leg toward quarter square triangle. Sew into seam allowance. Un-sew all stitches in the seam allowance. Press seam to left. Make 4.

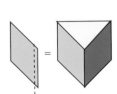

7. Sew 2-1/2" square to the right side of diamond assembly. Align top of square with top of diamond. The bottom of square will extend below diamond. Press toward diamond. Make 4.

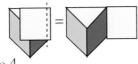

8. Using two assemblies from step 7, overlap them to sew the square to the other side of the diamond. Sew into the seam allowance. Un-sew all stitches in the seam allowance. Press seam toward diamond. Make 2.

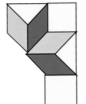

9. Fold the square in half along the diagonal, wrong sides together. Align edges of diamond. Pin the square so that it will not open (along the stitched sides). Sew from the beginning of diamond leg to end of diamond leg. Remove all stitches in the seam allowance. Press seam to the left. You should now have 1/2 of Lemoyne Star block. Make 2.

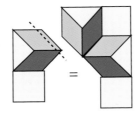
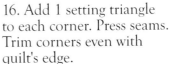

10. Using the 2 assemblies from step 9, sew diamond to square as in step 8. Sew into the seam allowance. Un-sew all stitches in the seam allowance. Press seam towards diamond.

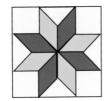

11. You should only have 1 seam to sew. Match centers and pin. Fold squares in half along the diagonal and pin together at sewn seams. Align edges of diamond and pin. Sew straight across and into both seam allowances. Un-sew all stitches in the seam allowance. Press seam open or spin in the same direction as the other diamond seams.

12. Square the Lemoyne Star block to 7-1/4". Make 9 blocks.

13. From the setting triangle fabic, cut (2) 5-3/4" strips. Using the strips, cut 12 setting triangles. To cut the triangles align the 45° line from your 24" rotary cutter ruler even with the top of the strip. Be mindful to maintain the 90° when making the second cut for each triangle.

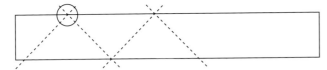

14. From the setting square fabric, cut (4) 7-1/4" squares.

15. Here's the fun part. Arrange the Lemoyne Stars, 4 background squares, and 8 setting triangles in position for the finished quilt. Assemble the quilt in diagonal rows as shown. Sew the rows together for the center area of the quilt. Press seams.

16. Add 1 setting triangle to each corner. Press seams. Trim corners even with quilt's edge.

17. Cut border fabric into (4) 4-1/2" x 42" strips. Sew the strips together end-to-end. Measure the quilt from top to bottom through the center of the quilt and cut (2) border strips equal to this measurement. Sew borders to both sides of the quilt.

18. Measure the quilt from side to side through the center of the quilt and cut (2) border strips equal to this measurement. Sew borders to the top and bottom of the quilt.

19. Layer backing, batting, and quilt top. Try machine quilting using rayon thread to give your quilt a shimmering dimension and a bit of sparkle. Quilt in an overall design.

20. Cut bright binding fabric into (4) strips 2-1/2" x 42". Sew strips together end-to-end. Fold strip in half lengthwise and press fold line. Align raw edges of binding to raw edges of quilt top. Sew in place. Turn folded edges to back of quilt and sew in place.

Passage of Time

The original 1930/40s' vintage quilt used a huge variety of plaids, checks, and stripes; with some florals and geometrics. This adds to the eclectic look of the quilt. If you don't usually use these fabrics, now is the time to try. It's fun and you don't need to worry about matching the lines.

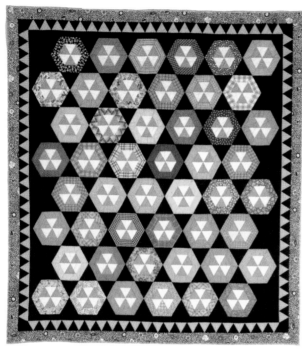

Quilt Size: 81" x 88"
Block Size: 12"
Block Count: 48
Quilted by Erin Underwood

Supplies:

3/4 yd fabric A; cut into 3-1/4" x 42" strips
3/4 yd fabric B; cut into 3-1/4" x 42" strips
48 2-1/4" x 42" assorted fabrics for outer round of hexagons
2 yd fabric C for setting pyramids, border #1 and border #2
3/4 yd fabric D for border #2
1 yd fabric E for border #3
2/3 yd for binding
4/5 yd fabric for backing and queen size batting

Special Tool:

60 Degree Triangle Ruler by Creative Grids™

Instructions:

1. Working with fabric A, layer multiple strips to speed cut. Use the 60 Degree Triangle Ruler and cut (3) pyramids for each Spider Hexagon block for a total of (144). Repeat with fabric B cutting additional triangles for a total of (144).

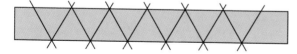

2. Working the the 2-1/4" strips (outer round fabric), cut (6) matching polygons for each Spider Hexagon block for a total of (288). Use the 60 Degree Triangle Ruler and align top of strip with 2-3/4" mark and bottom of strip with 5" mark.

3. Sew 3 pyramids of fabric A to the short edge of polygon. Repeat with fabric B. You should have 6 pieced pyramids: 3 wih fabric A and 3 with fabric B, all 6 with the same outer round fabric. Press seams of light pyramid units toward the polygon and seams of dark pyramid units toward the triangle.

4. Layout the pieced pyramids, alternating fabrics A and B. Sew together to form 2 half hexagons. Pin the seam at the center intersection and the beginning and ending of the half blocks before sewing to prevent stretching. The side edges are on the bias. Press seams.

5. Sew the 2 half block units together to make the Spider Hexagon block. Press final seam open. Make 48.

6. Cut approximately (4-5) 5" strips using fabric C. Cross cut using the 60 Degree Triangle Ruler for setting pyramids. (Cut 70). Using 2 pyramids, sew to each side of the Spider Hexagon as in the sketch. Press seams toward pyramid.

7. Layout the pieced Spider Hexagon blocks with attached background pyramids for the final placement in each row on a large surface. There will be 8 rows with 6 Spider Hexagon blocks in each row. Play with your arrangement until it is pleasing to your eye.

Sew the units together to form the rows. As you sew the row together you will find that pinning at all intersections and at the beginning and end of each seam will keep rows square.

Note: The Spider Hexagon is somewhat directional on how the pyramids in the center "wheel" are positioned. You want to be consistent on which sides of the Spider Hexagon you place the pyramid.

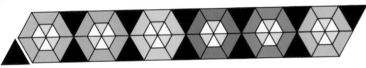

8. Unsew a pyramid from 1 end of the row and sew to the Spider Hexagon block at the opposite end.

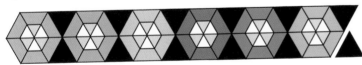

9. Use fabric C to cut (3) strips 6" x 42". Open strip to full width; cut triangles aligned to the 30° line on your 24" rotary cutting ruler; even with the top of the strip for the first cut. For the second cut, align the ruler of the first cut edge to the 60° line for each triangle, cutting about (3) from each strip.

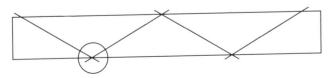

10. Insert the large triangles in 2 steps.

Pin the center of the large triangle to the center of the Spider Hexagon block. Gently lay the triangle down the full length of the seam and pin in position. When sewing, DROP the needle in the center of the triangle and stitch to the outside edge. Repeat for the other side of the triangle, always starting in the center and sewing to the outside edge. This will prevent bunching or pleating at the top center of the setting triangle. Press seams toward triangle. Add triangles to both sides of the quilt to square off the sides.

Note: The pyramids at the ends of the rows alternate from left to right as the rows are sewn together. The background pyramids form a star pattern when aligned correctly.

Add a pyramid to the two remaining corners at the top and bottom of the quilt to fill in the ends of the rows.

Trim the corners of the quilt to finish. Square off the quilt top.

11. For pieced border #2 cut (3) 3-1/4" strips from fabrics C and D using 60 Degree Triangle Ruler cut lots of pyramids.

12. Sew pyramids together alternating between fabric C and D. Press seams to one side. It's hard to gage the length of the strips. Compare what you've sewn to the quilt's center. You want to have at least 2 pyramids, fabric D, longer and wider than the center. Borders should end with a fabric C pyramid on both ends. Make 2 pieced side strips and 2 top and bottom strips. Trim ends of pieced borders to 90°. Measure the height of the pieced border; cut 4 end squares to this measurement from fabric C.

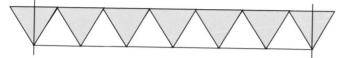

Border #1 is the floater border betwen the quilt's center and pieced border #2. To make a perfect fit based on your quilt, lay the quilt top and border sections on a flat surface.

13. Measure the following:

Dimension **A**: measure the quilt from top to bottom.
Dimension **B**: measure the length of one side of border #2.
Dimension **C**: measure the quilt from side to side.
Dimension **D**: measure the length of top/bottom border #2

At this point it is easier not to think about it, just do it.

14. The width of border #1 (sides) is (**D** minus **C** plus 1"), divided by 2 = _____ . This is cut width **E**.

15. Using fabric C cut (4) 42" long strips using the measurement of width **E**. Sew strips end-to-end. Cross cut (2) strips **A** long. Sew to the sides of the quilt top. Press seams towards border #1.

16. The width of border #1 (top and bottom) is (**B** minus **A** plus 1") divided by 2 = _____. This is cut width **F**.

17. Measure the quilt from side to side (quilt plus both side border #1 strips). This is length **G**. Using fabric C cut (3) 42" long strips using width **F**. Sew strips end-to-end. Cross cut (2) strips **G** long. Sew to top and bottom of the quilt. Press seams towards border #1.

18. Sew border #2 long pieced strips to each side of the quilt. Press seams towards border #1. Sew the fabric C cut squares to each end of border #2 top/bottom strips. Sew the borders to the top and bottom of the quilt and press seams toward border #1.

Border Measuring Diagram

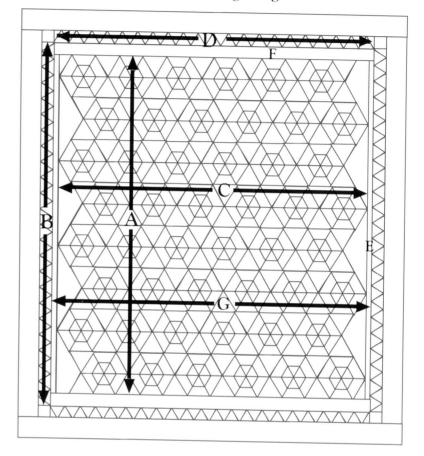

19. For border #3 cut (9) fabric E strips 3-1/2" x 42". Sew strips together end-to-end. Measure quilt from top to bottom; cut (2) strips to this length and sew to quilt sides.

20. Measure the quilt from side to side and cut (2) strips from the remainder of the long fabric E strip to this length. Stitch the strips to top and bottom of the quilt. Press seams towards border #3.

21. Layer the backing, batting and quilt top. Baste the layers together. Quilt as you like. Try machine quilting with a rayon thread to add a bit of shimmer. For hand quilting, experiment with quilting using #8 perle cotton in a utility stitch.

22. Cut binding fabric into (9) 2-1/2" x 42" strips. Sew together end-to-end. Fold in half lengthwise and press for a double fold binding. Match raw edges of binding to raw edges of quilt top. Stitch in place. Turn folded edge to back of quilt and stitch in place by hand or machine.

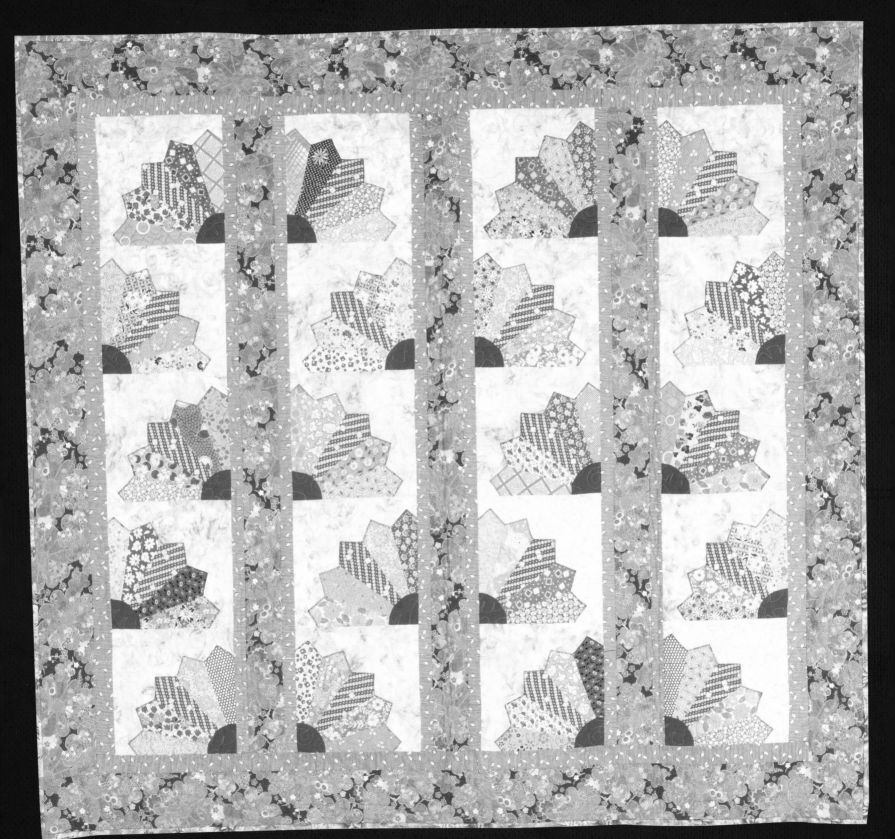

Tokyo Fans

The fan blades read mostly medium and don't show much contrast between blades. The dense large scale floral border makes a bold statement in this quilt. All other fabrics are the supporting cast.

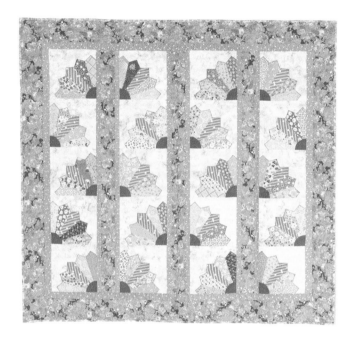

Quilt Size: 68" x 63"
Block Size: 10"
Block Count: 20
Quilted by Beth Hanlon-Ridder

Supplies:

Assortment of fabric for (100) fan blades (min. cut: 4" x 7")
1 fat quarter (22" x 18") for center fan blade
1 fat quarter (22" x 17") for quarter round
1-1/2 yd for background
1-1/2 yd for narrow sashing
2-1/2 yd for borders
4-1/2 yd for backing and binding

Special Tools:

18 Degree Dresden Plate Ruler by Creative Grids™
Straight pins

Instructions:

1. Cut strips 7" wide from each scrap. Using the 18 Degree Dresden Plate Ruler, cross cut fan blades aligning the 1" mark on the ruler even with the strip. The other side of the strip should be aligned with the 8" mark on the ruler. Continue cutting fan blades from an assortment of fabric until you have reached a total of (100).

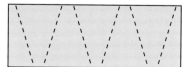

2. Fold each fan blade in half with right sides together, lengthwise. Sew across the "fat" end of the fan blade, finger press the seam open. Turn the fan blade right side out, then center the seam along the center of the fan blade. You just completed the "point" on the fan blade. Press flat. Repeat to make 100 fan blades.

3. Randomly select 2 fan blades, pair right sides together. Pin the beginning and end of the seam. Begin stitching at the point end. It is helpful to backstitch at the point end. Continue stitching to the end of the blade. Press seam open. Make 40 pairs.

4. Sew fan pairs to each side of a center fan blade. Press seams open. Make 20 fans.

5. Using the background fabric, cut (20) 10-1/2" squares. Position the fan on the background square aligning the outside edges. You should have a quarter round opening at the bottom corner of the block. Pin in place along the fan points and down the sides.

6. Thread sewing machine with two threads or a heavier weight thread in the top and one bobbin thread. You may need a "topstitch" needle to accommodate the extra thickness. Blanket stitch the points of the fan to the background square.

Option: You may trim out the background fabric from behind the fan block before sewing the round. Leaving it in place adds stability to the block since the fan blades are on the bias.

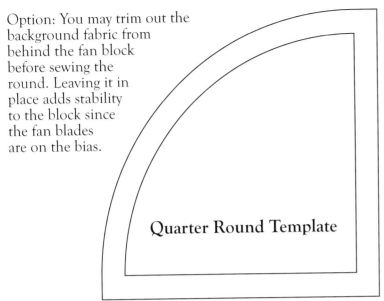

Quarter Round Template

7. Using template provided, cut (20) quarter round circles. Turn and press the 1/4" seam allowance on the curved edge and baste to hold. Position the quarter round on the fan block, aligning the corner and sides. Pin in position. Machine blanket stitch quarter round to the fan block along the curved edge. Remove basting.

8. Lay out the fan blocks in 4 vertical rows. Move the blocks around until you are pleased with the arrangement. Sew the blocks together in vertical rows. Press seams away from the fan's edge to reduce bulk. Make 4 rows. Measure the length of the rows (use average if necessary). This is Measurement **A**.

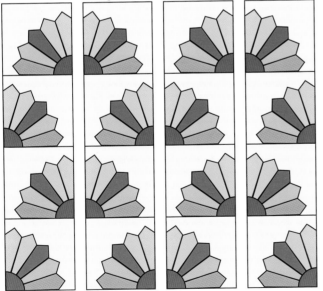

9. Using the narrow sashing fabric cut (9) strips 1-1/2" x 42". Cut (6) strips 2" x 42".

10. From the border fabric cut (4) strips 3-1/2"x 42". Cut (6) strips 5" x 42".

11. Sew the 1-1/2" sashing strips end-to-end for one long strip. Cut in half for (2) strips approximately 147" long.

12. Sew the 3" border fabric srips end-to-end for one long strip.

13. Sew the sashing to each side of the border strip. Pin before sewing to reduce stretching. Press seams toward sashing.

14. Cross cut this pieced assembly into 3 sections using Measurement A (from step 8). Sew between the 4 rows of fan blocks. Pinning will keep everything square and prevent stretching. Press seams toward sashing.

15. For border #1, sew together the (6) 2" strips of sashing fabric together end-to-end. Measure the quilt from top to bottom through the center of the quilt and cut (2) border strips equal to this measurement. Sew the borders to the sides of the quilt.

16. Measure the quilt from side to side through the center of the quilt and cut (2) border strips from the fabric for border #1 equal to this measurement. Sew the borders to the top and bottom of the quilt.

17. For border #2, sew the 5" strips together end-to-end. Measure the quilt from top to bottom through the center of the quilt and cut (2) border strips equal to this measurement and sew to the sides of the quilt.

18. Measure the quilt from side to side through the center of the quilt and cut (2) border strips from the fabric for border #2 equal to this measurement. Sew the borders to the top and bottom of the quilt.

19. Layer the quilt backing, batting, and quilt top. Baste the layers together. Quilt as you like. Mine is quilted in a thread color that matched the background fabric. It was quilted on a longarm machine with a lovely continuous ginkgo leaf pattern.

20. Cut remainder of backing/binding fabric into (7) 2-1/2" x 42" strips. Sew together end-to-end. Fold in half lengthwise and press for a double fold binding. Match raw edges of binding to raw edges of quilt top. Stitch in place. Turn folded edge to back of quilt and stitch in place.

Carnival

Big wheels keep on turning...so why do they call this Feathered Star? I'm always fascinated by block names and how they got them. This block was really fun to piece which is probably why this collection contained 25 blocks. Give it a try and don't let the curves intimidate you.

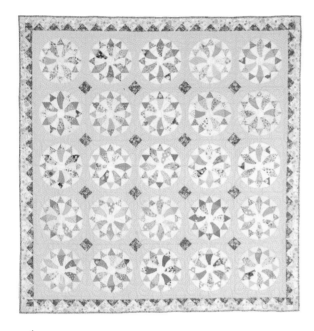

Quilt Size: 83" x 83"
Block Size: 14-1/2"
Block Count: 25
Quilted by Beth Hanlon-Ridder

Supplies:

14 assorted fat quarters for feature fabrics
1-1/4 yd for feathered star background
1 yd accent fabric for corner triangles and border #2
4-1/2 yd for block background and border #1
1-1/4 yd fabric for borders #2 and #3
2/3 yd binding fabric
Heat resistant template material, cotton swabs, liquid starch

Special Tool:

Companion Angle Ruler™ by Wrights

Instructions:

Set Up: Transfer templates A, B, and C to lightweight card stock. Cut out to include seam allowances.

1. Trace and cut out (6) pieces A on the wrong side of feature fabric. Trace and cut out (6) pieces A on wrong side of star background fabric. Sew pieces together alternating between the feature fabric and the star background fabric. Press seams clockwise. This is ring #1.

2. Cut out center circle D from star background fabric. Trace inside circle of circle D template onto heat resistant template material. Cut out. Using liquid starch and cotton swab; wet the seam allowance around the outside edges of fabric circle. Using the side of a dry iron set to medium, press the circle's seam allowance over the edge of the heat resistant template. Allow to cool, then remove the template. Applique the circle to the center of ring #1.

3. Trace and cut out (12) pieces B onto feature fabric. Trace and cut out (12) pieces C onto star background fabric. Sew together, alternating between feature fabric and star background fabric. Make sure you are sewing the straight sides and not the arc edges. Press seams counter clockwise. This is ring #2.

4. Align ring #1 with ring #2 making sure the wedge shape is directly over the cylindrical shape. Pin in place and sew rings #1 and #2 together. Press seams. Make 25 blocks.

5. Cut a 15" square from background square. Fold in quarters to mark center of square on each side. Measure completed Feathered Star circle. Cut a circle which is 1" less in diameter than the Feathered Star block. Cut 25 background squares.

6. Align the Feathered Star points with the fold lines on the block background square. Pin and ease in the remaining fullness. Sew and press seams toward background square.

7. Cut (4) strips 2-1/2" from the corner triangle accent fabric; cross cut (64) 2-1/2" squares . Mark diagonal line on each square. Place square on the corner of block background fabric. Sew on diagonal line to form the corner triangles. Trim excess 1/4" from stitched line. Place corner triangles as follows:
   9 blocks - all four corners
   12 blocks - two corners
   4 blocks - one corner

8. Follow diagram for layout; the corner triangles form squares on point when the blocks are sewn together.

9. Using border #2 accent fabric, cut (5) 2-1/2" strips; cross cut (72) quarter triangles using the Companion Angle Ruler and cut (4) 2-1/2" x 2-1/2" corner squares.

10. Using border #2 and #3 accent fabric, cut (5) 2-1/2" strips; cross cut (76) quarter triangles using the Companion Angle Ruler.

11. Sew quarter square triangles on the short side alternating between border #2 accent fabric and border #2 and #3 fabric. Begin and end with border #2 and #3 fabric triangles. Make (4) strips with (18) accent triangles. Square ends of each strip leaving 1/4" seam allowance beyond the accent triangles.

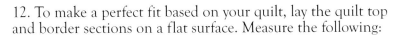

12. To make a perfect fit based on your quilt, lay the quilt top and border sections on a flat surface. Measure the following:

Dimension **A**: measure the quilt from top to bottom.
Dimension **B**: measure the length of one side of border #2.
Dimension **C**: measure the quilt from side to side.
Dimension **D**: measure the length of top/bottom border #2

13. At this point it is easier not to think about it, just do it.

The width of border #1. (**D** minus **C** plus 1"), divided by 2 = _____ . This is cut width **E**.

Using border #1 fabric cut (4) strips using width **E**. Sew strips end-to-end. Cross cut (2) strips **A** long. Sew to the sides of quilt top. Press towards border #1.

The width of border #1 (**B** minus **A** plus 1") divided by 2 = _____. This is cut width **F**.

Measure the quilt from side to side (quilt plus both side border #1 strips). This is length **G**. Cut (3) strips using width **F**. Sew strips end-to-end. Cross cut (2) strips **G** long. Sew to top and bottom of the quilt. Press towards border #1.

14. Sew border #2 pieced side strips to each side of the quilt. Press seams towards border #1. Sew the 4 corner squares from step 9 to both ends of the top and bottom border #2 pieced strips. Sew border #2 pieced strips to the top and bottom of the quilt. Press seams toward border #1 to complete the quilt top.

Border Measuring Diagram

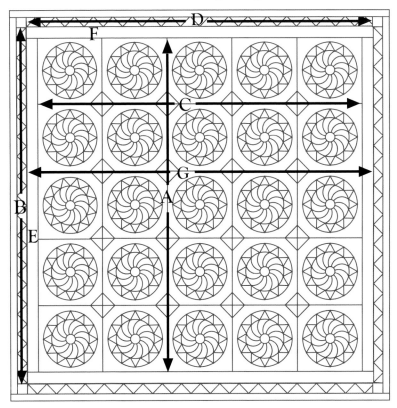

15. Using fabric for border #2 and #3 cut (9) strips 2" x 42" and sew together end-to-end. Measure the quilt from top to bottom through the center of the quilt and cut (2) border strips equal to this measurement. Sew the borders to the sides of the quilt. Measure the quilt from side to side. Cut (2) strips to this measurement and sew to the top and bottom of the quilt..

16. Layer the quilt backing, batting, and quilt top. Baste the layers together. Quilt as you like. Mine is quilted on a longarm machine in a swirl design with a gold color cotton thread.

17. Cut binding fabric into (9) 2-1/2" x 42" strips. Sew together end-to-end. Fold in half lengthwise and press for a double fold binding. Match raw edges of binding to raw edges of quilt top. Stitch in place. Turn folded edge to back of quilt and stitch in place.

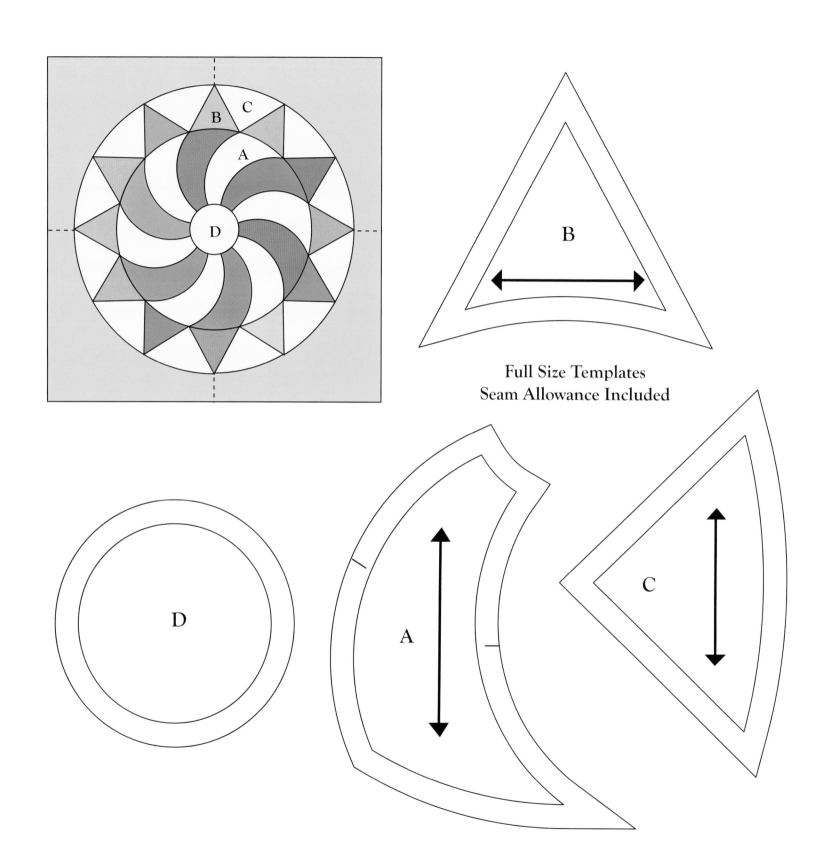

Full Size Templates
Seam Allowance Included

Resources

QUILT SERVICES

I would not have considered starting this journey without the help of these four talented, professional, longarm-machine quilters. There is no question about their skill and artistry as quiltmakers and designers. They advised, sketched, and researched quilting designs that would unify and enhance each quilt with quiet splendor. They know threads, fibers, and batting and are pros at what will be quilted out and what will be quilted in. They create miracles.

Johanna Roll
c/o ROLL FINISHER
410-452-5234

Peg Dougherty
c/o TIMELY STITCHES
pegndavedou@wildblue.net
410-452-5646

Beth Hanlon-Ridder
c/o THE STUDIO ON HARVEST FARM
harvestfarm@comcast.net

Erin Underwood
c/o MY MACHINE QUILTER
erin@mymachinequilter.com
www.mymachinequilter.com

Vintage quilts, tops, blocks, and lots of antique linens in all sorts of conditions are plentiful...in my quest for quality goods I relied on my personal shopper, Barbara.

VINTAGE TEXTILES MADE NEW
Barbara Herron, Owner
oldtextilesmadenew@yahoo.com

Rail Fence ❖ 96" x 96" ❖ QUILTMAKER: **Flo Lincoln**

QUILTING SUPPLIES

The two shops listed below are well stocked and have a delightful staff. You can find them on the web, at the major quilts shows, or you can visit their stores. Both give exceptional service and never run low on energy. They have my favorite specialty rulers made by Creative Grids™ and EZ Quilting® by Wrights® and also the newer quilt washes. I've tried Restoration™ Fabric Restorer, Soak™ Fabric Wash, and Fairfield QuiltCare Quilt Wash with much success. The new washes are gentle and fragrance-free yet have unbelievable ability to remove stains, lift dirt, and brighten colors.

CREATIONS SEWCLEVER
Rita Fishel, Owner
192 S. Paint St
Chillicothe, OH 45601
1-888-SEW-CLVR
www.creationssewclever.com

GRUBER'S QUILT SHOP
Sue Poser, Owner
310 4th Avenue NE
Waite Park, MN 56387
1-877-778-7793
www.grubersquiltshop.com

When you need books about block names and dating fabric the one stop shop is Quilting Books Unlimited. They have 243 books listed on their reference/history web pages. I do enjoy shopping in their booth during quilt shows to see all their import books on Japanese, Welsh, British, and Australian quiltmaking.

QUILTING BOOKS UNLIMITED
Rob Roberts and Betty Boynik-Roberts, Owners
13772 Cottage Drive
Grand Haven, MI 49417
1-800-347-3261
www.qbu.com

Acknowledgements

Certainly *Quilts* would not have had that personal connection to all families without the wonderful black and white photographs that friends so graciously provided. Because they were "good" friends, some went out of their way to obtain the photographs by cajoling their moms. Sometimes they had to almost pledge their lives to guarantee their safe return. The photographs were indeed family treasures and I enjoyed each story that was shared. They reflected on people no longer with us. They provided wonderful memories of family events and traditions with lots of hugs, laughter, and tears. The photographs told tales of cotton candy, country living, silly games, vacations at the beach, and all things that seemed to be so much bigger than life. We were, by most accounts, very small when the photographs were taken so everything looked big to us and we had no worries. Life from that perspective was grand. With that, I humbly thank the following friends for entrusting me with original photographs from their family albums.

Barbara Polston, Chicago, IL

Barbara Jean Schwarz Herron, Woodstock, VA

Phyllis Brown and Ophelia Scales, Portsmouth, VA

Jeanne Armstrong Foster, Lancaster, PA

LuJuana Jones Richardson, Portland, OR

Fonzora and Eugene Fitzgerald, Philadelphia, PA and Taiwan, China

Louise and Gene Umbarger, Churchville, MD

Denise Diggs Kirkland, Baltimore, MD

Irene and Charles Greene, Brooklyn, NY

Edward J. and Edith A. Presberry, Darlington, MD

Doretha Estell Green, Monticello, AR

Linda Laskey Brand, Bradley Beach, NJ

Jean Ann Wright, Flint, MI and Palm Beach, FL

Bob and Bobbi Compton, Red Bank, NJ

Yoshiko McCrory, Osaka, Japan

Bob and Kris Pelletier, Manchester, CT

Kathryn Gamble, Cheshire, MA

Suzanne Shreve, Panama Canal Zone, Panama

Elizabeth Lane-Stevens, Chicago, IL and Harlem, NY

I am blessed and thankful to have Rhonda M. Adams in Alexandria, Virginia as a friend and fellow quiltmaker. Rhonda was kind enough to proof the pattern for Spider Hexagon and her beautiful quilt graces the cover of this book.

Then there is that marvelous estate known as Federal Hill Farm in Street, Maryland belonging to Bob and Bobbi Compton. The gardens were perfect the day of the photo shoot and the weather could not have been better. I am thankful that it was also a perfect day for golf so Bob would not have to witness and cringe as ladders and nails went in unthinkable places. Special thanks go to Bobbi for her unending support and for being extremely accommodating.

Last, but certainly not least, I would like to thank Barbara Herron and Beth Hanlon-Ridder. They were with me from the beginning, through the middle, and at the finish. They gave me energy to continue through my lows and cheered with me when things were soaring.

There are so many more I could name as each friend touched, changed, or managed my world so I could focus over the past two years. You kept my path clear, thank you.

Also Available

The Dream
A Magical Journey in Colourful Stitches

Price: $29.95

ISBN: 978-0-9768215-1-9

Poetry & Patchwork

Price: $12.95

ISBN: 978-0-9768215-2-6

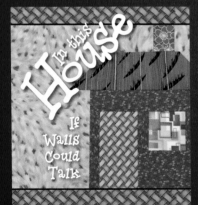

In this House

Price: $5.95

ISBN: 978-0-9768215-3-3

LECTURES/ WORKSHOPS

Gyleen is absolutely passionate about quilting and haiku poetry! Visit her on the web for patterns, note cards, and books, to schedule your group for her interactive lectures or workshops, or sign up for her free e-newsletter.

ORDERING INFORMATION

FPI Publishing books are available online or at your favorite bookstore.

For More Information, Visit: **www.ColourfulStitches.com**

About the Author

Gyleen was born in Philadelphia, Pennsylvania, grew up in Taiwan and Japan and now calls Maryland her home. She obtained a Bachelor of Science degree in Chemical Engineering at Drexel University.

Her quilts blend colour, pattern and texture providing a contemporary essence to traditional quilting. Her written works center on haiku poetry, quilt patterns, magazine articles, and the crème de la crème, children's books. *The Dream: A Magical Journey in Colourful Stitches*, her first children's book, brings together the written word with the visceral comfort of quilts. As a quilt artist she has achieved "Best of Show" recognition; as a writer, her journey is just beginning.

Lone Star ❖ **90" round** ❖ ESTATE OF: **Esther C. de Lashmutt**